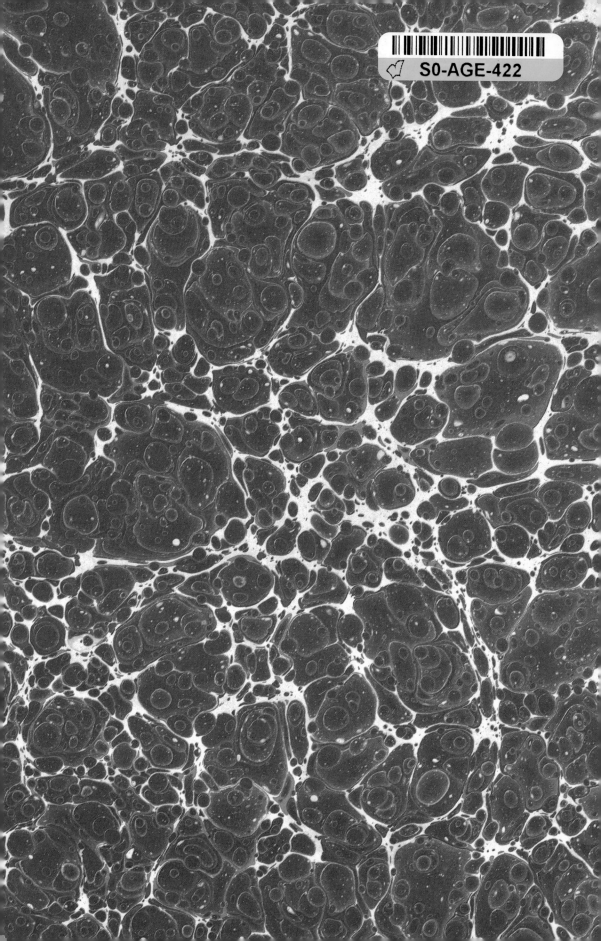

To Bob & Mary Ellen
From
Paul & Lois
7/89

DECOYS

of the mid-Atlantic region

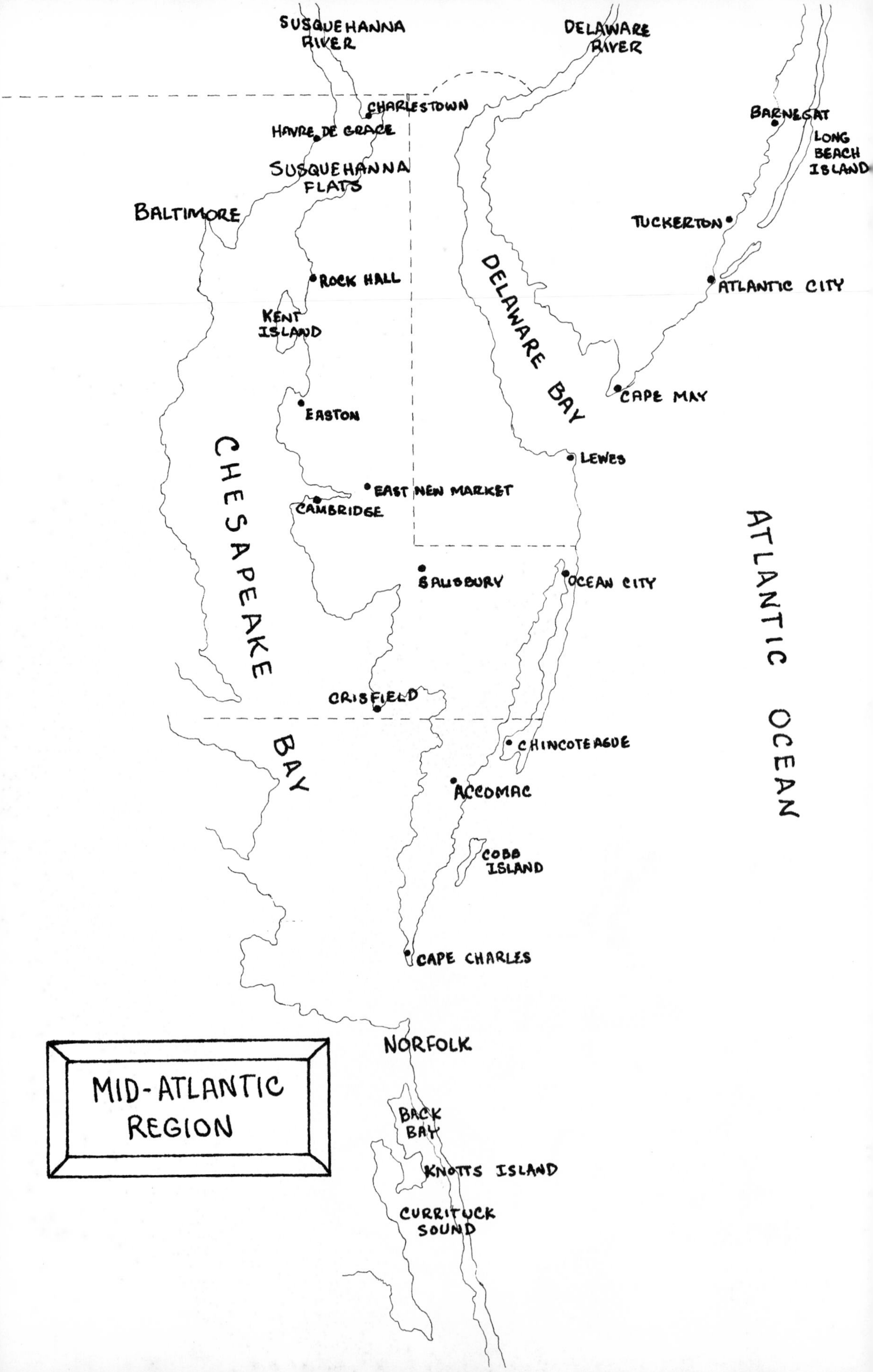

SUSQUEHANNA
RIVER

DELAWARE
RIVER

CHARLESTOWN

HAVRE DE GRACE

BARNEGAT

LONG
BEACH
ISLAND

SUSQUEHANNA
FLATS

BALTIMORE

TUCKERTON

DELAWARE BAY

ROCK HALL

ATLANTIC CITY

KENT
ISLAND

EASTON

CAPE MAY

CHESAPEAKE

LEWES

EAST NEW MARKET

CAMBRIDGE

SALISBURY

OCEAN CITY

ATLANTIC OCEAN

CRISFIELD

BAY

CHINCOTEAGUE

ACCOMAC

COBB
ISLAND

CAPE CHARLES

NORFOLK

BACK
BAY

MID-ATLANTIC
REGION

KNOTTS ISLAND

CURRITUCK
SOUND

DECOYS

of the mid-Atlantic region

Henry A. Fleckenstein, Jr.

Schiffer Publishing Ltd

Box E, Exton, Pennsylvania 19341

iv

Library of Congress catalog card number: 79-52438

ISBN: 0-916838-24-2

Printed in the United States of America

For Barbara, Josh, and Katie

PREFACE   ix

CHAPTER 1.   HISTORY   13

CHAPTER 2.   NEW JERSEY COAST   19

CHAPTER 3.   DELAWARE RIVER   57

CHAPTER 4.   SUSQUEHANNA FLATS   79

CHAPTER 5.   CHESAPEAKE BAY   139

CHAPTER 6.   EASTERN SHORE OF VIRGINIA,
              BACK BAY-CURRITUCK SOUND   189

CHAPTER 7.   MAKERS   229

CHAPTER 8.   COLLECTING, RESTORATION
              AND VALUES   253

              SUGGESTED READING   261

              PICTURE CREDITS   263

              BIBLIOGRAPHY   265

              INDEX   267

Charles Barnard, circa 1910.

Preface

The Eastern Shore of Maryland is an enchanting place to live. For one who has lived in the country all of his life and loved every minute of it, it is fitting to now be settled in the delightfully rural county of Dorchester on Maryland's Eastern Shore. Settling in the tiny town of East New Market, which is situated in the center of a supremely rich agricultural mother lode that produces a great wealth of crops and in turn provides abundant cover and food to many kinds of wildlife, has allowed me to enjoy country living similar to that which I remember as a boy. Only a mile from home courses the beautiful Choptank River, so named for the tribe of Indians that once roamed its shores. The large twisting body of water with its innumerable guts and marshes provides, along with the grain fields planted adjacent, an irresistable lure to the migratory waterfowl that each fall fill the skies of the Atlantic flyway.

There are a number of similar extraordinarily attractive rivers that empty into the renowned Chesapeake Bay on the Eastern Shore of Maryland. One such river forms part of the watery boundaries of Kent Island in Queen Anne's County, a short distance north of where I live now in East New Market. It was here at Love Point on the Chester River, only a short distance from where I spent my early youth, that my deep impassioned interest in wooden decoys awakened. The year was 1960 and my brother, a friend, and I were hunting out of a blind not 100 yards from where my father ran his rowboat rental business in the years after the war and where my brother and I used to watch the old "Smoky Joe" ferry dock on its trip from Baltimore. The day was beautiful, sunny and warm, not at all the blustery icy kind of weather that only a duck hunter can appreciate and a duck can enjoy. Understandably the fowl were not trading. Rather than doze in the blind, I decided to stroll along the brush laden shore line of the river in hopes of jump shooting an unwary black duck. There are few people who can stroll the shores of a large bay without kicking and poking through the immensely interesting conglomerate of storm tossed flotsam that trades one shore for another, from one river to the other, during each blow. Who knows what treasure might be hiding in these masses of everything that floats, even if it be only an interesting piece of driftwood. As I walked I looked — for anything. Climbing through the branches of a huge tree that had eroded into the river, I caught a glimpse of something moving up ahead of me. When I peered around the root mass of the next tree across my path, I saw a pair of canvasbacks. It was immediately obvious that they were decoys, lying askew in only a couple of inches of water up against some broken branches. Now here was a find, thought I, something to be retrieved and slung over the shoulder by their still attached anchor weights and strings. What a nice addition they would make to our rig of plastic and styrofoam decoys riding at anchor back in front of the blind.

By that time I had walked quite some distance up the shore and as the afternoon was drawing short, I headed back to the blind and my companions. They were as happy as I with the new decoys. They certainly enhanced our meagre rig and seemed to add a bit of respectability to it. They did seem to ride the slightly chopping waters of the Chester River a good deal more realistically than their plastic counterparts. The two wooden birds, one hollow and one solid, floated deeper and bounced less than the others. I remember thinking at that time that they were antiques and really shouldn't be used, and I wondered aloud to my brother if maybe Dad had made these very birds back in the forties when we had lived just up the road from where we were now hunting. My father had made a few decoys then to help a friend of his, a man who I later learned was Phil Kemp, a local handyman and guide who lived at Miss May's Hotel on Love Point and took parties from Baltimore duck hunting out of his blind offshore from the ferry docks. Dad was a waterman and a gifted craftsman — he and my uncle built some of the finest cypress skiffs that ever floated on the Chester River — and when he wasn't fishing, crabbing, or building boats, he would help Phil Kemp guide his parties and make decoys. Dad's production was limited though, because he only shot fowl we needed to eat, and decoys were unnecessary for the kind of hunting that my father enjoyed. He took my brother and me occasionally, we were about 5 and 6 years old then, and I believe my love for waterfowl and the pursuit of them traces back to those early years. Dad would wait for a full moon in October or November by which time the northern black ducks and Canada geese would have arrived in our area and would be using the local corn fields in good numbers. The three of us would make our way to the woods after dark, follow our path to the edge of a large field, one which had a generous pile of ear corn suspiciously close to our hide, and snuggle down into the honeysuckle. In those days, it didn't take long before a usually wary black duck or two would drop in to feed on the late night snack which had been provided for them. What seemed to be an abnormally loud blast would shatter the peaceful but excitedly anticipatory moment. The gunshot would reverberate across the corn fields from the Chester River to the Chesapeake Bay and then all would be silent. Our dinner for the following evening would be corn fed black duck.

At the end of our hunting trip that winter day in 1960, the two wooden decoys were picked up with the rest of the rig, thrown into the back of the truck and carried home. Later that week I was showing Dad the wooden ducks that I had found and he said he believed there were several decoys out back in the shed that had been brought along when we moved to Harford County from the Eastern Shore in 1950. His remark that I was welcome to them if I could find them under all of the junk was the only incentive I needed to clean out the sheds. A short time later I had added five more wooden decoys to my already expanding collection. What a motley crew they were, but I was excited and the bug had definitely bitten.

Living in Harford County even just a short twenty years ago was the right place to live for a new collector with limited resources. There were plenty of decoys in antique shops, sporting goods stores and at the local Saturday night auctions. They ranged in price up to $2.50 each, a considerable sum for an old wooden duck decoy that wasn't to be used to lure ducks anymore. My collection grew fast, and along with my natural interest in history, it sparked the most fascinating aspect of decoy collecting that I have discovered in the past twenty years — the study of that decoy, its history, its maker, and its place in the events that occurred during its functional life. Original paint, aesthetic appeal, whether it is folk art or not are secondary considerations and are very often the capricious whims of individuals who accumulate decoys; but the history and the enjoyment of the research for that history are what appeal to the real decoy student.

Those who spend hours or months trying to determine whether their decoy has its original paint or not are not interested in the decoy as much as they are in whether they have made a wise investment . . . Those who argue as to which decoy has the most graceful lines or the most stylish head are more interested in whether or not that decoy will look nice on the mantle in their family room; and those who are solely concerned with whether this piece is truly folk art or not should stick to collecting cigar store Indians.

These observations are surely going to offend some of my decoy collecting friends, and although I certainly respect and understand their interests and reasons for collecting, it's difficult for me to believe that they are getting any real feeling for the essence of the decoy.

Almost twenty years of collecting has not dimmed my enthusiasm for decoys, and although my one time avocation has developed into a full time vocation, I am still a collector first. I hope this literary endeavor will provide some spark of interest to all people interested in decoys, whether they be historians, collectors, acquisitors, or investors. I have enjoyed writing it and I have learned a great deal in the process.

I would like to thank a few of my good friends for their help and their permission to photograph their collections for inclusion in the book. My sincere and warmest thanks to my personal friends Bobby Richardson, John Hillman, Larry Lambert, and Bill Walsh who extended their time and hospitality at their homes and made available their extensive collections and information; to my enthusiastic and erudite friend, George Reiger, for his encouragement, advice, and the use of a superb decoy from his collection; to my hometown friend, John Sullivan of Bon Air Farm in Fallston who provided access to his collection of early Harford County papers that aided my research on the history chapter; and a special thanks with love to my proofreader and typist who has put up with serving dinner on the coffee table for too many months.

East New Market, Maryland   Henry A. Fleckenstein, Jr.
        April 30, 1979

CHAPTER 1

History

The wooden decoy is a truly original American art form. Although in the beginning, its use was strictly functional, during its making it allowed the creative urges that lie dormant in most men to surface. The artistic expressions in wood that were the result are sought today by a whole new population of collectors. Now, centuries after the first wooden decoy was made, it is taking its rightful place in the ever increasing realm of collectible native American art.

The earliest constructed decoys were made by the first Americans, the Indians. In 1924 eleven decoys were discovered in the now well known archaeological digs at the Lovelock Caves in Lovelock, Nevada. Estimates of their age have ranged from 1000 to 2000 years old. They were made by the ancestors of the Paiute Indians out of tule rushes bent and woven into the proper form of the canvasback. They had actual white feathers stuck in their sides and back, and reddish brown and black dyes added the finishing touches of color for the head, breast, and tail areas. The representation of the canvasback duck was thus captured perfectly and it is certain that these earliest of decoys performed as well than as their wooden counterparts would a thousand years later.

More than enough has been written of the history of the first wooden decoys in America, but an attempt will be made here to briefly list the facts in chronological order tracing this record. It will provide all that is needed by the beginning collector, whose first exposure to decoys may be this book.

Joel Barber's book *Wild Fowl Decoys,* first published in 1934, was the original book on decoys. It has been republished several times and is still in print today. In it Mr. Barber relates the story of a ledgendary tale written in 1842 by a local gunner on Long Island about his great-grandfather's gunning experiences. The account goes into some detail concerning the great-grandfather's duck shooting over wooden decoys. Figuring the great-grandfather's time as three generations preceding would date these possibly first wooden decoys to sometime before the American Revolution.

The next account mentioning wooden decoys is in the book, *Alexander Wilson Naturalist and Pioneer,* a biography by Robert Cantwell published in 1961. In a story on hunting mallards it is told how Wilson and his friends used carved decoys in 1796, along with a boat to drift into the rafting ducks in a manner similar to that used on the Delaware today.

In line with this period Adele Earnest has two eighteenth century carvings in her collection. Both of them are pictured in her book, *The Art of the Decoy,* published in 1965, and Miss Earnest states they date from the eighteenth century. One is a fully carved bird that bears very little resemblance to a working duck decoy and the other bird is a primitive Long Island root head merganser. Documented pieces this early are very rare and are an important addition to any collection.

Of the same approximate age as these examples, Mr. Barber has a drawing in his book of a Long Island decoy that dates to about 1800 and was made by a man named Ben Hawkins.

Next we progress to the year 1801-1814 and the publication of Alexander Wilson's first edition of *Wilson's American Ornithology* in which he has described methods of hunting wild ducks. Included in this is information concerning the use of wooden figures carved and painted to imitate ducks, and sunk to the proper depth with ballast weights made of lead nailed to the bottom. These decoys were then set out on the ponds frequented by the fowl while the hunter who placed them lay waiting in ambush on the shore.

A few other references are made to decoys and their use in various shooting stories and manuals that were published during the period from 1820 to 1850. Much of it was written and published in England by Englishmen who had tried their hand at waterfowl shooting in America. Very little information on hunting was published or written at this time in this country, because Americans had not begun to relax to the point where they could engage in hunting for sport. They certainly didn't have time to write about it, consequently few records exist for this period. The hardy individuals who did hunt waterfowl, for the most part, were providing sustenance for their families. The market that would demand wild game for food in later years had not yet come of age. This later demand for wild game and the need to supply the markets of Baltimore, Philadelphia, and New York, along with the advent of the faster, more reliable breech loading shot guns, gave birth around the middle of the nineteenth century to the market hunter.

At about this same time, sport hunting among the wealthy became popular all along the mid-Atlantic coast and the demand for and development of the decoy progressed rapidly.

In *Krider's Sporting Anecdotes* published in 1853 stories are told of battery or sinkbox shooting on the Upper Chesapeake Bay and mention is made of the great numbers of wooden ducks that were used. It is quite natural that the earlier history of the decoy is related to the Chesapeake Bay, as there were more ducks shot there than in any other location in America. Every waterman, bayman, hunter, or fisherman who enjoyed duck shooting, whether it was one bird for the evening stew pot or one hundred birds for the city markets, made decoys. From Barnegat to Currituck, each designed to the specific needs of their own particular areas, decoy making flourished.

Four men who lived in the heart of the waterfowl rich areas of the Atlantic seaboard probably made more decoys in their lifetimes than were made by all the other makers in all the other regions of the country combined. They were Harry V. Shourds of Tuckerton, New Jersey, Samuel T. Barnes of Havre de Grace, Maryland, William Heverin of Charlestown, Maryland and Ira Hudson of Chincoteague, Virginia. Premier collectible decoys in fine original conditions made by each of these men are still available to today's collectors.

Through the fantastic duck shooting years of the seventies, eighties, nineties, and into the early years of the twentieth century, many thousands of decoys were chopped, whittled, sanded, and painted. While men sailed their ships, had their hair cut, tended fish nets, kept watch at lighthouses, and whiled away any other unused hours, they made their working wooden tools, creating unknowingly someone's later day treasure.

By today's standards, prices of decoys back then seemed inexpensive — the 1895 Harford County, Maryland tax assessment records show the 500 decoys of the San Domingo Club on the Gunpowder River assessed at $100 and their goose and swan decoys at $6.00 — even so, they were a valuable and indispensable part of any hunter's outfit. Without his rig of decoys, where would he be? Therefore many decoy owners took precautions to protect their investment. A number of the early rigs of individuals and clubs were branded with the person's name or the club name in the bottom of the decoys. They were branded for the purpose of identification

"Daddy" Holly decoy circa 1875 showing round iron keel and the brand "Reckless" a sailing scow on the flats.

so that if they got away from their owner in any manner, their eventual return would be facilitated. This elementary safeguard prevented many decoys from straying very far from their rightful owners. It is true that some rigs were still stolen and the owner suffered a personal setback, but these decoys were not gone forever. They were sold off to another hunter in another area and were soon put back into the service for which they were intended. Under other circumstances, when decoys broke loose from their anchors during blustery storms and floated farther down the river or bay to be tossed up on some strange shore amongst the flotsam, they were seldom lost for very long. Most of the time they were retrieved by another hunter and were soon seeing duty on new waters. When I was a boy living at Love Point, Maryland on Kent Island, we would walk along what we called Bay Shore after a violent blow and often pass strings of tangled decoys, only to leave them lay, as we excitedly searched the newly eroded cliffs along the shoreline for the numerous Indian arrowheads and axeheads to be found there. How I would love to be able to return to those times and redirect my collecting efforts.

Still other decoys had their heads or bills broken off as a result of the rough handling they were often subjected to, and normally broken things might be discarded, but every man who hunted back then could whittle a head. The broken heads were easily replaced and the decoy again became a member of the rig. Hundreds of decoys exist today with early bodies and later heads replaced by other makers.

The only decoys truly lost for all time during that early period were those destroyed in a fire, when some hapless gunner's shed or barn would burn to its foundation. Fire would reduce the vulnerable wooden ducks to ashes. These decoys would have to be replaced.

The point being made in the preceding paragraphs, is that of the tens of thousands of decoys made before 1920 very few were lost for the future generations of collectors.

Of course with the sale of all migratory wildfowl declared illegal in 1918, things changed. Hunting for the market was now an occupation of the past and the need for the huge rigs of decoys diminished. There was a surfeit of decoys wherever waterfowl shooting occurred. The city market no longer demanded the large numbers of wild ducks, or any at all for that matter. It was against the law to sell them. Many men, market hunters and decoy makers in particular, were out of work; and they turned to what they knew best for employment, the waters on which they lived. Many of them fished, clammed, or crabbed, and others took to guiding the "sports" from the cities to support their families. Sport gunning continued to be a popular past-time after the sale of migratory fowl was outlawed. There were still good populations of ducks and geese and bag limits were high enough to make it worthwhile to go to the trouble and expense of duck shooting.

Many hundreds of decoys continued to be made in the areas where they were always made. Sink box gunning was not prohibited in Maryland until 1935 and it was not uncommon to rig out a box in the 1920's with 300 or more decoys. Bushwhacking was also a common method of duck shooting on the Susquehanna Flats and a hundred or more decoys are required for a successful bushwhacking rig.

On the Susquehanna Flats many rigs of decoys were sold down the bay when the sink box was finally outlawed in 1935. To be sure many were sold in the same manner in 1918 after the migratory bird act was passed. It is not unusual to rig out a hundred or more decoys today on parts of the Chesapeake Bay even with the severely reduced limits with which we are faced. In the twenties, thirties and forties every prominent point or sheltered cove on the Bohemia, Sassafras, Chester, Choptank, Honga, Pocomoke, Potomac, Patuxent, Severn, Magothy, Back, Middle, Gunpowder, and Bush Rivers had a duck hunting blind that required a large rig of decoys to lure the birds. These are just some of the major rivers that empty into the Chesapeake. Multiply this by all the other principal hunting areas in the mid-Atlantic region and one can see there was still a great need for large numbers of wooden decoys.

No, the multitudes of duck decoys did not pass out of existence completely when hunting for the market ended. The need, though lessened, was still there and it is against the nature of most Americans to get rid of anything. We are incorrigible hoarders. For every decoy that was thrown into a flaming bonfire, or was used to fill a ditch, or was split into kindling, or burned in a wood stove, or was thrown away, or given away, or allowed to float away down the river, there were ten, or maybe a hundred, stacked, probably not too carefully in sheds, barns, cellars, attics, and even boat houses to lay through the years until today. And thousands of those decoys are still there waiting for collectors like you and I to finally discover them.

CHAPTER 2

New Jersey Coast

All along the New Jersey coast, the prevalent type of decoy is referred to, by collectors everywhere, as the Barnegat Bay style or the "dugout" style. This reference stems from the fact that most all of the decoys made along the coast are similar to the ones made by the decoy makers that lived around the head of Barnegat Bay; that is, clean and simple of line, two piece hollow construction, light in weight and tending toward the small side.

The decoys of the most noteworthy maker in New Jersey, those of Harry Van Nuckson Shourds of Tuckerton, are exemplary models of this design. Although he lived and worked farther down the coast on the waters of Little Egg Harbor, his birds are perfect examples of the ultimate New Jersey decoy.

As the Barnegat Bay sneak boat was developed through the years for hunting on Jersey waters, so the Barnegat Bay decoy evolved for use in conjunction with this boat. The pattern for the boat called for a small lightweight type that could be easily pulled up onto the marsh for concealment by one man. The smaller and lighter the decoys used, the more birds one man could carry in his sneakboat. The Jersey decoys are almost uniformly made of white cedar that grows locally in the meadows that line the Jersey coast. Commonly referred to as swamp cedar, it is a very light, close grained wood that is easily worked and extremely durable and resistant to checks or cracks if properly seasoned. Due to its former abundance and the skilled craftsmen who carefully selected it, the wood in many of the early Jersey decoys found today has withstood the rigors of bay gunning through the years remarkably well. Cracks and splits are more likely found in the pine heads than the cedar bodies. Only a few New Jersey coast decoys are known that are not hollow two piece construction. They were hollowed by hand gouging tools for the most part and a small gouge type hammer known as a dugout tool was developed in this area to perform a lot of the work. Some of the makers used wood chisels and still others used a drill press such as was used by the Mason Decoy Company for hollowing.

The bodies were finished generally in a rounded pattern with a distinct tail usually in the middle of the body except on species such as Canada geese and brant which had a high tail. There was no incised carving on the birds except in the bill area, and here many makers carved nostrils, mandible separations, and nails on the end of the bill. The only relief carving shows up as a shoulder separation in the form of a deep gouge chiseled behind the neck and extending part way into the back on decoys by some makers. A few Jersey coast decoys have flat bottoms but most have well rounded bottoms that go along with the general rounded appearance.

All of the New Jersey decoys I have handled have been weighted with lead in one form or another, and the majority have been rectangular or square pads of lead attached to the bottom of the decoy with small nails or screws. Several of the makers who worked in the area of Tuckerton and Manahawkin cut beveled rectangular slots into the bottom of their birds and then poured hot lead into the opening. This latter method of weighting the decoys helped maintain the clean pure lines so characteristic of this area.

The universal manner of attaching the anchor line to the decoy in New Jersey seems to have been the leather thong as most all decoys examined from this region that are in original condition have the leather thong.

The many previously published statements that New Jersey coast decoys are big headed seem unfounded to this writer as the majority of the birds appear beautifully proportioned in size and their conformation is nearly perfect in most instances.

The characteristically refined style of the decoys made up and down the Jersey coast along with the availability of the names and history of the makers add up to a very pleasing wooden bird that is avidly sought by collectors all over the country.

Hen and drake oldsquaw circa 1890 — Harry V. Shourds, Tuckerton, New Jersey — original paint. The ultimate in rare and valuable decoys, this pair of hollow carved old squaws number among only a few that are known by Shourds.

Redhead drake circa 1890 — Harry V. Shourds, Tuckerton, New Jersey — original paint — mint condition.

Black duck circa 1910 — Jesse Birdsall, Barnegat, New Jersey — original paint — hollow carved white cedar.

Hen and drake oldsquaw circa 1880's — Mark English, Somer's Point, New Jersey — original paint. A rare and beautiful pair of South Jersey hollow "dugouts." Rig of Harry Boice, Pleasantville, New Jersey.

Hen and drake red-breasted mergansers circa 1905 — Harry V. Shourds, Tuckerton, New Jersey — original mint paint and condition.

Upper: Drake and hen red breasted merganser circa 1890 — Applegate Family, Bayville, New Jersey — original paint.

Middle: Drake and hen red breasted merganser circa 1890 — Henry Grant, Barnegat, New Jersey — original paint.

Lower: Drake and hen red breasted merganser circa 1910 — Mason Decoy Company, Detroit, Michigan — original paint. Mason decoys such as these excellent birds were used all over the country.

Upper: Drake and hen red breasted merganser circa 1930's — Rowley Horner, West Creek, New Jersey — original paint by Chris Sprague.

Middle: Drake and hen red breasted merganser circa 1880 — Mark Kear, Linwood, New Jersey — original paint.

Lower left: Drake red breasted merganser circa 1920's — Amos Doughty Absecon, New Jersey — original paint.

Lower right: Drake red breasted merganser circa 1890 — maker unknown, Tuckerton, New Jersey — original paint.

Upper left: Drake red breasted merganser circa 1930's — Charles Huff, Shrewsbury, New Jersey — original paint.

Upper right: Drake red breasted merganser circa 1920's — Clark Madieri, Pittman, New Jersey — original paint.

Middle: Drake and hen red breasted merganser circa 1900 — Lloyd Parker, Parkertown, New Jersey — original paint. Outstanding original specimens of the very finest New Jersey coast work.

Lower: Hen and drake red breasted merganser circa 1900 — Rhodes Truex, Absecon, New Jersey — original paint.

Drake and hen bufflehead circa 1910 — Jake Barrett, Somers Point, New Jersey — original paint.

Upper: Drake red breasted merganser circa 1880 — Bill Hammel, Absecon, New Jersey — original paint.

Middle: Hen red breasted merganser circa 1880 — Bill Hammel, Absecon, New Jersey — original paint.

Lower: Hen red breasted merganser circa 1900 — Mark English, Somers Point, New Jersey — original paint.

Upper: Two drake goldeneyes circa 1890 — Clark Madieri, Pittman, New Jersey — original paint — Hazelhurst Club rig.

Middle left: Drake goldeneye circa 1930 — Gene Hendrickson, Lower Bank, New Jersey — original paint.

Middle right: Drake goldeneye circa 1900 — maker unknown, Tuckerton area, New Jersey — original paint.

Lower: Drake and hen goldeneye circa 1940's — Clark Madieri, Pittman, New Jersey — original paint.

Upper: Hen and drake bufflehead circa 1880 — John English, Florence, New Jersey — original paint.

Middle: Drake and hen goldeneye circa 1890 — Jesse Birdsall, Barnegat, New Jersey — old repaint.

Lower: Drake and hen scaup circa 1890 — Harry V. Shourds, Tuckerton, New Jersey — original paint.

Upper left: Redhead drake circa 1890 — Harry V. Shourds, Tuckerton, New Jersey — original paint.

Upper right: Redhead drake circa 1890 — Harry V. Shourds, Tuckerton, New Jersey — Bonnett Club paint.

Middle left: Redhead drake circa 1930's — John Updike, Greenbank, New Jersey — original paint.

Middle right: Redhead drake circa 1890 — Henry Kilpatrick, Barnegat, New Jersey — original paint.

Lower left: Redhead drake circa 1890 — Taylor Johnson, Point Pleasant, New Jersey — original paint.

Lower right: Redhead drake circa 1930's — Stanley Grant, Barnegat, New Jersey— original paint. Son of Henry Grant.

Upper: Drake and hen scaup circa 1920 — Cliff Cane, Beach Haven, New Jersey — original paint.

Middle: Drake and hen scaup circa 1945 — Dan Kingsley, Point Pleasant, New Jersey — original paint.

Lower left: Redhead drake circa 1940's — I. S. Hankins, Point Pleasant, New Jersey — old repaint.

Lower right: Scaup drake circa 1940's — Joe King, Edgley, Pennsylvania — original paint.

Upper left: Scaup drake circa 1890 — Charles McCoy, Tuckerton, New Jersey — original paint.

Upper right: Goldeneye drake circa 1920's — Will Hall, West Mantoloking, New Jersey — original paint.

Middle: Drake and hen American goldeneye circa 1890 — Harry V. Shourds, Tuckerton, New Jersey — original paint. An exceptionally rare pair of decoys.

Lower: Drake and hen scaup circa 1890 — Taylor Johnson, Point Pleasant, New Jersey — original paint.

Upper: Drake and hen mallard circa 1930's — Rowley Horner, West Creek, New Jersey — original paint. A superb decoy in mint condition.

Middle: Drake and hen scaup circa 1930's — Rowley Horner, West Creek, New Jersey — original paint — near mint.

Lower: Drake and hen goldeneye circa 1930's — Rowley Horner, West Creek, New Jersey — original paint. A lovely little pair of decoys.

Upper left: Redhead drake circa 1900 — Lloyd Parker, Parkertown, New Jersey — original paint.

Upper right: Red head drake circa 1890 — Bill Hammel, Absecon, New Jersey — original paint.

Middle: Drake and hen goldeneye circa 1900 — Harry Mitchell Shourds, Ocean City, New Jersey — original paint.

Lower: Drake and hen redhead circa 1900 — Lloyd Parker, Parkertown, New Jersey — original paint.

Upper left: Drake scaup circa 1930's — John Updike, Greenbank, New Jersey — original paint.

Upper right: Drake scaup circa 1920's — Taylor Johnson, Point Pleasant, New Jersey — original paint.

Middle left: Redhead drake circa 1890 — Eugene Birdsall, Point Pleasant, New Jersey — original paint.

Middle right: Redhead drake circa 1890 — Taylor Johnson, Point Pleasant, New Jersey — original paint.

Lower left: Hen scaup circa 1920 — Lou Barkelow, Forked River, New Jersey — original paint.

Lower right: Hen scaup circa 1920's — Stanley Grant, Barnegat, New Jersey — original paint.

Upper left: Black duck circa 1930 — Rhodes Truex, Absecon, New Jersey — original paint.

Upper right: Black duck circa 1930 — Rowley Horner, West Creek, New Jersey — original paint.

Middle: Black duck circa 1930's — John Updike, Greenbank, New Jersey — original paint.

Lower left: Black duck circa 1910 — Taylor Johnson, Point Pleasant, New Jersey — original paint.

Lower right: Black duck circa 1900 — Clark Madieri, Pittman, New Jersey — original paint.

Upper left: Black duck circa 1925 — Harry Mitchell Shourds, Ocean City, New Jersey — old repaint.

Upper right: Black duck circa 1930 — Rhodes Truex, Absecon, New Jersey — original paint.

Middle: Black duck circa 1890 — Brad Salmon, Manahawkin, New Jersey — original paint.

Lower left: Black duck circa 1890 — Henry Grant, Barnegat, New Jersey — original paint.

Lower right: Black duck circa 1890 — Ellis Parker, Long Beach Island, New Jersey — original paint.

Upper left: Black duck circa 1930 — John Updike, Greenbank, New Jersey — original paint.

Upper right: Black duck circa 1930 — John Updike, Greenbank, New Jersey — original paint.

Middle left: Black duck circa 1900 — Henry Grant, Barnegat, New Jersey — original paint.

Middle right: Black duck circa 1930's — Rowley Horner, West Creek, New Jersey — original paint by Chris Sprague.

Lower left: Black duck circa 1890 — Lloyd Parker, Parkertown, New Jersey — original paint.

Lower right: Black duck circa 1890 — Bill Brown, Parkertown, New Jersey — original paint.

Upper: Drake and hen black duck, circa 1925 — Dominic Sabatini, South Jersey — original paint.

Middle: Two black ducks, circa 1920 — Clark Madieri, Pittman, New Jersey — repaint by Lem Ward.

Lower left: Black duck, circa 1890 — maker unknown, South Jersey — old repaint.
Lower right: Lesser scaup circa 1900 — maker unknown, Barnegat, New Jersey area — original paint.

Upper left: Black duck circa 1920's — Harry Mitchell Shourds, Ocean City, New Jersey — original paint.

Upper right: Black duck circa 1920's — Harry Mitchell Shourds, Ocean City, New Jersey — original paint — rare swimming head.

Middle: Black duck circa 1920's — Harry Mitchell Shourds, Ocean City, New Jersey — original paint.

Lower left: Black duck circa 1890 — Harry V. Shourds, Tuckerton, New Jersey — original paint.

Lower right: Black duck circa 1890 — Harry V. Shourds, Tuckerton, New Jersey — original paint.

The above decoys represent a good study of Shourds black ducks.

Note: All birds on this page are made of hollowed white cedar from the Jersey meadows.

Upper: Drake and hen goldeneye circa 1920's — Stanley Grant, Barnegat, New Jersey — original paint. Died 1960.

Middle: Black duck circa 1920's — J. W. Bowen, Atlantic City, New Jersey — original paint.

Lower left: Black duck circa 1880 — attributed to Joe King, Manahawkin, New Jersey — old repaint.

    Note: Mr. John Hillman, noted authority on New Jersey decoys, believes this bird could have been made by Liberty Price, Parkertown, New Jersey circa 1880. Further research in the future could prove this point.

Lower right: Black duck circa 1910 — Mark Kear, Linwood, New Jersey — old repaint.

Upper left: Drake scaup circa 1930's — Harry V. Shourds, Tuckerton, New Jersey — original paint.

Upper right: Drake scaup circa 1880 — Dodge Decoy Company, Detroit, Michigan — original paint.

Middle: Hen red breasted merganser circa 1875 — maker unknown, Barnegat, New Jersey — original paint.

Lower left: Drake scaup circa 1930's — Rhodes Truex, Absecon, New Jersey — old repaint.

Lower right: Drake scaup circa 1950's — Willis Johnson, Lakewood, New Jersey — original paint.

Upper: Redhead drake circa 1890 — Harry V. Shourds, Tuckerton, New Jersey — original paint.

Middle: Hen and drake scaup circa 1910 — Harry V. Shourds, Tuckerton, New Jersey — original paint.

Lower: Black duck circa 1890 — Harry V. Shourds, Tuckerton, New Jersey — original paint.

Upper: Black duck circa 1920's — Harry Mitchell Shourds, Ocean City, New Jersey — original paint.

Middle: Drake and hen scaup circa 1920's — Harry Mitchell Shourds, New Jersey — original paint.

Lower: Redhead drake circa 1920's — Harry Mitchell Shourds, Ocean City, New Jersey — original paint.

Upper: Drake and hen scaup circa 1920 — Harry Mitchell Shourds, Ocean City, New Jersey — original paint.

Middle: Drake and hen scaup circa 1900 — Henry Grant, Barnegat, New Jersey — original paint.

Lower left: Redhead drake circa 1880 — attributed to Joe King, Manahawkin, New Jersey — original paint.

> **Note:** Mr. John Hillman, noted authority on New Jersey decoys, believes this bird could have possibly been made by Liberty Price, Parkertown, New Jersey, circa 1880. Further research in the future could prove this point.

Lower right: Scaup drake circa 1920's — Stanley Grant, Barnegat, New Jersey — original paint.

Upper: Brant circa 1920 — Rowley Horner, West Creek, New Jersey — original paint.

Middle: Brant circa 1920's — Lou Cranmer, Manahawkin, New Jersey — original paint.

Lower: Brant circa 1920's — Lou Cranmer, Manahawkin, New Jersey — original paint.

Upper: Brant circa 1890 — Harry V. Shourds, Tuckerton, New Jersey — original paint.

Middle: Brant circa 1890 — Lloyd Parker, Parkertown, New Jersey — original paint.

Lower: Brant circa 1890 — Lloyd Parker, Parkertown, New Jersey — original paint.

Upper: Brant circa 1890 — Joe King, Manahawkin, New Jersey — original paint.

Middle: Brant circa 1910 — Sam Forsyth, Bay Head, New Jersey — bird restored by John Hillman.

Lower: Brant circa 1930's — Chris Sprague, Beach Haven, New Jersey — original paint.

Upper left: Brant circa 1965 — Harry Shourds III, Seaview, New Jersey — original paint — hollow white cedar construction.

Upper right: Brant circa 1950's — maker unknown, Barnegat area, New Jersey — original paint — hollow.

Middle: Brant circa 1950's — Gene Hendrickson, Lower Bank, New Jersey — original paint — hollow.

Lower left: Black duck circa 1920 — Harry Mitchell Shourds, Tuckerton, New Jersey — old "flocked" repaint — hollow.

Lower right: Lesser scaup circa 1955 — Dipper Ortley, New Jersey — original paint — hollow.

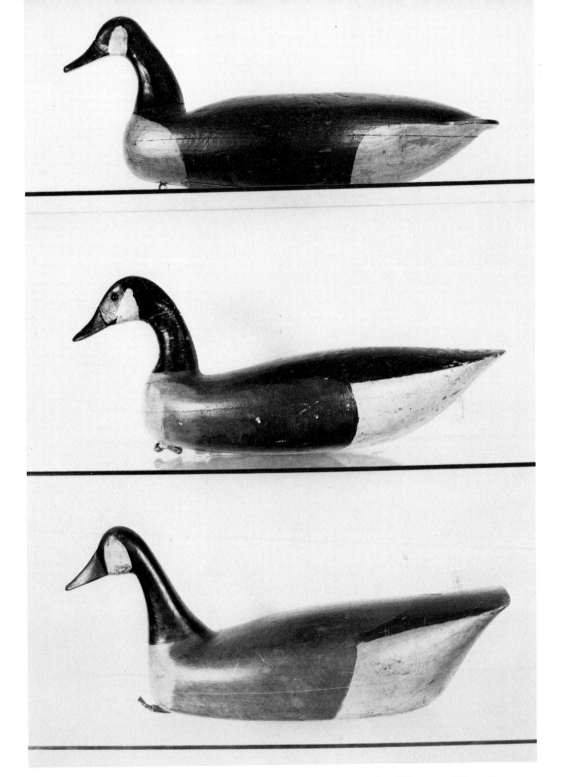

Upper: Canada goose circa 1885 — Taylor Johnson, Point Pleasant, New Jersey — original paint.

Middle: Canada goose circa 1910 — Harry Mitchell Shourds, Ocean City, New Jersey — original paint.

Lower: Canada goose circa 1930's — Chris Sprague, Beach Haven, New Jersey — original paint.

Upper: Canada goose circa 1900 — Lloyd Parker, Parkertown, New Jersey — original paint.

Middle: Canada goose circa 1890 — Henry Kilpatrick, Barnegat, New Jersey — old repaint.

Lower: Canada goose circa 1910 — Rhodes Truex, Absecon, New Jersey — original paint.

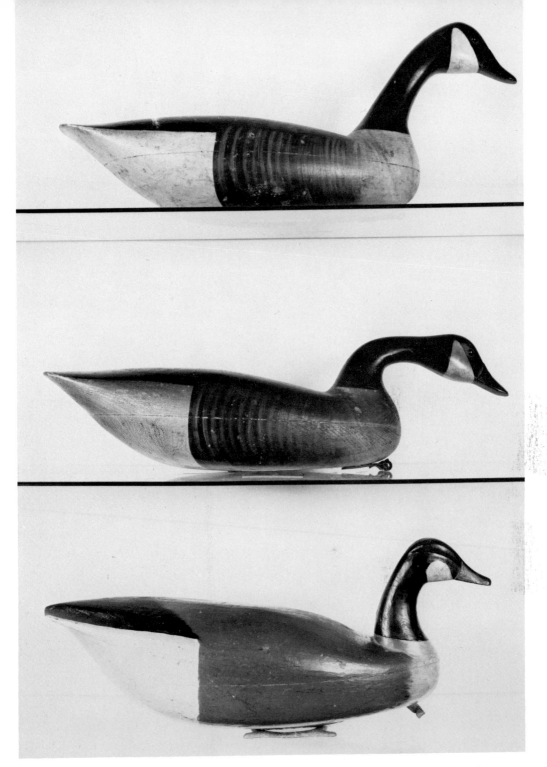

Upper: Canada goose circa 1920 — Harry V. Shourds, Tuckerton, New Jersey — original paint. A great Canada goose decoy.

Middle: Canada goose circa 1920 — Harry V. Shourds, Tuckerton, New Jersey — original paint — feeding or swimming head position. An exceptional decoy.

Lower: Canada goose circa 1880 — Jesse Birdsall, Barnegat, New Jersey — original paint.

Upper: Canada goose circa 1890 — John Dorsett, Point Pleasant, New Jersey — original paint.

Middle: Canada goose circa 1890 — Henry Grant, Barnegat, New Jersey — original paint.

Lower: Canada goose circa 1890 — Roy Maxwell, Wading River, New Jersey — original paint.

Upper: Brant circa 1910 — Rhodes Truex, Absecon, New Jersey — original paint.
Middle: Brant circa 1880 — possibly John Inman, Manahawkin, New Jersey — old repaint.
Lower: Canada goose circa 1900 — J. W. Bowen, Atlantic City, New Jersey — original paint.

CHAPTER 3
Delaware River

All collectors seem to like Delaware River black duck decoys. There is a certain fineness about the carving and painting style that attracts everyone and it seems that when a collector mentions Delaware River, most people think of the black duck. Yet there were decoys made and used along the river for many different species, and the Blair pintail and mallard decoys are probably among the finest birds that ever floated the Delaware. The early history of decoy making along this river is obscure and vague; Alexander Wilson hunted mallard and black ducks over decoys by an unknown maker as early as the last quarter of the eighteenth century. And some of the Blair decoys were made in the 1860's according to Joel Barber, but the facts of the Blair decoys are shrouded in mystery. No one seems to know for sure who made them, who painted them, or where or when they were made. One thing is sure, a definitive study is needed and perhaps some collector from that area is doing the necessary research at this moment.

Most of the information that is known and recorded about the makers on the Delaware River dates after 1900 and many of the decoys documented today were made during the period 1900-1950.

These later dates, the care with which the smaller rigs were handled, and the fact that most all of the hunting was done in fresh water account for the very good condition of a lot of Delaware River decoys that are in collections at this time. The paint in nearly all cases is slightly stylized and often is the first coat. Most of the makers spent considerable effort on their feather painting and the result on the black duck is particularly pleasing. In addition incised feather carving on the back and tail add to the effectiveness and pleasant appearance. Most bodies have a well rounded design with a full, extended breast and in many cases are further adorned with raised and carved wing tips. Some others appear squarish in a profile view but always with rounded edges. Almost all Delaware River birds are of hollow two piece construction and many have heads tucked down on their breasts in a restful attitude. Those birds used farther down the river toward the Delaware Bay seldom exhibited the raised wing or incised tail carving so common up river.

The particular method of hunting on the Delaware, that of sculling downriver onto the birds after they have alighted in the decoys, required extremely realistic stool that appeared contented and thus would fool the wild ducks into remaining in position until the hunter arrived.

The many fine beautifully carved specimens of the decoys that remain to grace collectors' shelves provide visible proof that these makers along the Delaware knew their wild ducks well.

Goldeneye drake circa 1885 — John English, Florence, New Jersey — original paint. This decoy portrays well English's stylized feather carving in the back and tail.

A head-on view of the preceding bird showing the extreme narrowness of old man John English's heads.

Pintail drake circa 1870 — John Blair, Philadelphia, Pennsylvania — original paint. A beautiful bird with exquisite grace showing the mastery of this maker.

Left: Drake green wing teal circa 1890 — Blair school, Delaware River — original paint.
Right: Drake blue wing teal circa 1890 — Blair school, Delaware River — original paint.

Upper left: Black duck circa 1925 — John Heisler, Bordentown, New Jersey — original paint.

Upper right: Black duck circa 1925 — John Heisler, Bordentown, New Jersey — original paint.

Middle left: Black duck circa 1925 — John Heisler, Bordentown, New Jersey — original paint.

Middle right: Black duck circa 1890 — John English, Florence, New Jersey — original paint.

Lower left: Black duck circa 1900 — J. Baker, Edgley, Pennsylvania — original paint.

Lower right: Black duck circa 1910 — Tom Fitzpatrick, Delanco, New Jersey — original paint.

Upper left: Black duck circa 1920 — Dan English, Florence, New Jersey — original paint.

Upper right: Black duck circa 1925 — Joe King, Delaware River — original paint.

Middle: Black duck circa 1920's — William Quinn, Yardley, Pennsylvania — original paint.

Lower left: Black duck circa 1930's — William Quinn, Yardley, Pennsylvania — original paint.

Lower right: Black duck circa 1930's — William Quinn, Yardley, Pennsylvania — original paint.

Upper: Black duck circa 1870 — Blair style, Delaware River — original paint.
Middle left: Black duck circa 1930's — maker unknown, Delaware River — original paint.
Middle right: Black duck circa 1950's — Lawrence McGlaughlin, Edgley, Pennsylvania — original paint.
Lower: Black duck circa 1920's — John Heisler, Bordentown, New Jersey — original paint.

Upper left: Black duck circa 1930 — Richard Anderson, Delaware River — original paint.

Upper right: Black duck circa 1940's — Reggie Marter, Delanco, New Jersey — original paint.

Middle left: Black duck circa 1932 — Paul Green, Yardville, New Jersey — original paint.

Middle right: Black duck circa 1925 — John Heisler, Bordentown, New Jersey — original paint.

Lower left: Drake scaup circa 1925 — Dan English, Florence, New Jersey — original paint.

Lower right: Drake scaup circa 1930's — Lawrence McGlaughin, Edgley, Pennsylvania — original paint.

Upper left: Black duck circa 1890 — Ellis Parker, Long Beach Island, New Jersey — original paint.

Upper right: Black duck circa 1890 — Ellis Parker, Long Beach Island, New Jersey — old repaint.

Middle left: Black duck circa 1910 — Al Reitz, Croyden, Pennsylvania — original paint.

Middle right: Black duck circa 1920's — Reggie Marter, Delanco, New Jersey — original paint.

Lower left: Black duck circa 1920's — Jack English, Florence, New Jersey — original paint.

Lower right: Mallard circa 1890 — John English, Florence, New Jersey — original paint.

Upper: Hen and drake blue wing teal circa 1890 — of the Blair school, Delaware River — original paint.

Middle: Pintail drake circa 1870 — John Blair, Philadelphia, Pennsylvania — original paint. The rarest of the rare, only a handful of these decoys are known in collections today.

Lower: Black duck circa 1890 — Blair school, Delaware River — original paint — obviously made by the same hand as the teal above.

Upper: Hen red breasted merganser circa 1930's — John Dawson, Trenton, New Jersey, Duck Island — original paint.

Middle: Hen canvasback circa 1930's — John Dawson, Trenton, New Jersey, Duck Island — original paint.

Lower: Drake mallard circa 1930's — John Dawson, Trenton, New Jersey, Duck Island — original paint.

Upper: Drake and hen baldpate circa 1930's — John Dawson, Trenton, New Jersey, Duck Island — original paint.

Middle left: Black duck circa 1930's — John Dawson, Trenton, New Jersey, Duck Island — original paint.

Middle right: Drake redhead circa 1830's — John Dawson, Trenton, New Jersey, Duck Island — original paint.

Lower: Drake and hen pintail circa 1930's — John Dawson, Trenton, New Jersey, Duck Island — original paint.

Upper: Pintail drake circa 1920's — Tom Fitzpatrick, Delanco, New Jersey — original paint.

Middle: Gadwall drake circa 1940's — William Quinn, Yardley, Pennsylvania — original paint — very rare species.

Lower: Drake and hen red breasted merganser circa 1912 — Sam Archer, Bordentown, New Jersey — original paint.

Upper: Mallard hen circa 1940's — William Quinn, Yardley, Pennsylvania — original paint.

Middle: Mallard drake circa 1940's — William Quinn, Yardley, Pennsylvania — original paint.

Lower: Pintail hen circa 1940's — William Quinn, Yardley, Pennsylvania — original paint.

Upper left: Baldpate drake circa 1940's — William Quinn, Yardley, Pennsylvania — original paint.

Upper right: Baldpate hen circa 1920's — John Heisler, Bordentown, New Jersey — original paint.

Middle: Pintail drake circa 1930's — Joe King, Delaware River — original paint.

Lower: Pintail drake circa 1940's — John McGloughlin, Bordentown, New Jersey — original paint.

Upper: Hen and drake mallard circa 1940's — John McGloughlin, Bordentown, New Jersey — original paint.

Middle: Drake and hen blue wing teal circa 1950's — Reggie Marter, Delanco, New Jersey — original paint.

Lower left: Hen scaup circa 1930's — John McGloughlin, Bordentown, New Jersey — original paint.

Lower right: Pintail drake circa 1910 — maker unknown, Delaware River.

Upper left: Drake scaup circa 1910 — Joe King, Delaware River — original paint.

Upper right: Drake scaup circa 1900 — Dan English, Florence, New Jersey — old repaint.

Middle left: Drake scaup circa 1910 — William Quinn, Yardley, Pennsylvania — original paint.

Middle right: Drake scaup circa 1910 — William Quinn, Yardley, Pennsylvania — original paint.

Lower left: Drake scaup circa 1890 — Dan English, Florence, New Jersey — original paint.

Lower right: Drake redhead circa 1900 — Dan English, Florence, New Jersey — repaint by English in 1958.

Upper: Drake and hen scaup circa 1930's — Charles Huff, Shrewsbury, New Jersey — original paint.

Middle: Drake and hen scaup circa 1910 — John Roberts, Cape May, New Jersey — Delaware River type — original paint.

Lower left: Drake redhead circa 1890 — John English, Florence, New Jersey — original paint.

Lower right: Hen scaup circa 1920 — Dan English, Florence, New Jersey — original paint.

Drake and hen canvasback circa 1920's — John Heisler, Bordentown, New Jersey — original paint. Not many canvasback decoys of this quality were made for use on the Delaware River.

Upper: Canvasback drake circa 1932 — Paul Green, Yardville, New Jersey — original paint.

Middle: Scaup drake circa 1900 — Dan English, Florence, New Jersey — original paint.

Lower left: Scaup drake circa 1930's — Jack English, Florence, New Jersey — original paint.

Lower right: Scaup drake circa 1900 — John English, Florence, New Jersey — original paint.

Upper left: Bufflehead drake circa 1940's — Percy Gant, Osbourneville, New Jersey — original paint.

Upper right: Bufflehead drake circa 1890 — Harry V. Shourds, Tuckerton, New Jersey — original paint — Hazelhurst Club rig. An extremely rare and fine little decoy.

Middle left: Scaup hen circa 1930's — Paul Green, Yardville, New Jersey — original paint.

Middle right: Scaup hen circa 1910 — Al Reitz, Croyden, Pennsylvania — old repaint.

Lower left: Drake canvasback circa 1930's — Lawrence McGlaughlin, Edgley, Pennsylvania — original paint.

Lower right: Drake canvasback circa 1920 — Charles Allen, Bordentown, New Jersey — original paint.

Upper: Drake and hen goldeneye circa 1920 — Jake Barrett, Somers Point, New Jersey — original paint.

Middle: Black duck circa 1920 — William Quinn, Yardley, Pennsylvania — original paint.

Lower: Hen and drake mallard circa 1900 — Tom Fitzpatrick, Delanco, New Jersey — original paint.

Upper: Drake canvasback circa 1920 — Dan English, Florence, New Jersey — original paint.

Middle: Drake scaup circa 1920 — Dan English, Florence, New Jersey — original paint.

Lower left: Drake scaup circa 1920's — Cooper Berkley, Fieldsboro, New Jersey — original paint.

Lower right: Drake goldeneye circa 1890 — John English, Florence, New Jersey — original paint.

CHAPTER 4

Susquehanna Flats

As one thinks of the black duck when the Delaware River is discussed, the mere mention of the Susquehanna Flats brings to mind one bird, the canvasback. It was here on the Susquehanna Flats that market hunting flourished from the 1860's right on through to 1918 when the sale of all wildfowl was proscribed and the end to the slaughter of the canvasback was at hand. Up until that time market hunting was a way of life to the men who lived in the towns and villages that ringed this famous body of water. The machine of destruction, so to speak, was the sinkbox or battery which required large numbers of decoys to be used effectively. Rigs of as many as 500 decoys were not uncommon. Even as late as 1933, two years before the use of the sinkbox was declared illegal in Maryland, there were 30 of these devices licensed on the Susquehanna Flats. The great demand for the huge quantities of decoys needed in this one area along the Atlantic Flyway caused most of the men to turn to making wooden birds not only for their own use, but for the use of their neighbors. Simple logic proves that tens of thousands of decoys were made here during the hey day of gunning for the market.

The names of the towns that nestle on the shores of the Flats are becoming more familiar to decoy collectors across the country. It is no longer difficult to associate the names Holly, Barnes, McGaw, Lockard, Heverin, or Dye with the towns of Havre de Grace, Northeast, Charlestown, or Perryville. As more information is recorded and disseminated to the collecting public, interest in adding good examples of these makers' handiwork to the collector's shelves increases.

Historical writings bring one as close to the time when the use of decoys was instituted on the Susquehanna Flats as is possible in today's research.

There is a fine line drawn through this early era that one must endeavor to follow. Where documented information leaves off and personal interpretation and theory begin is where the extreme fineness of the above mentioned line is most evident. Even then it is abstruse. To date, no one has come forward to declare his attempt at such an examination or to publish his essay. This brief introduction to the Susquehanna Flats is not the proper place to chronicle fifteen years of definitive study on the decoy history of this area, but presenting a few facts here will be in keeping with the rest of the book.

In detailed accounts of canvasback shooting on the Chesapeake written in the 1830's little mention is made of the use of decoys, mostly only stories of pass shooting from points or bars of land extending out into the water. The infrequent use of a method known as "toling" whereby a dog that is trained to gambol on the banks of the waters in view of rafting wildfowl and thus lure them, out of curiosity, into the range of hunters hidden in the bushes, is mentioned. Apparently, from information contained in writings, the waterfowl abounded in such multitudinous numbers that decoys were unnecessary.

It is believed at some point during the 1840's that the sinkbox was introduced on the Susquehanna Flats by the market hunters from New York. It is very probable that decoys were in use at this time on the Flats by commercial hunters already living here. Dr. Elisha J. Lewis in his book, *The American Sportsman*, published in 1855, states that in the season beginning in 1846, the sinkbox, then called a surface boat, replaced the dugout, a small hollowed out skiff which was moored out on the feeding grounds of the ducks, concealed with eel grass, and surrounded by large numbers of anchored decoys. He further states that this dugout boat had been in general use on our bay and rivers for many years. Many years seems likely to have been at least ten years and possibly more, which would place the use of the decoy on the Susquehanna Flats to about 1835.

Dr. Elisha Lewis, Dr. J. J. Sharpless, and John T. Krider, all of Philadelphia, and Henry Dwight Chapin of Baltimore were all early American sporting writers that penned experiences of canvasback shooting on the Susquehanna Flats from about 1826 to 1855. Mention is made, in their books, of local Havre de Grace and Port Deposit gunners named Donahue, W. W. Levy, J. W. McCullough, Ben Davis, Baird, Charles Boyd, and John Holly. Of these names only John Holly is recognizable to persons interested in decoys. He was the famous "Daddy" Holly and John Krider writes that in the spring of 1850, John Holly, then 32 years of age, killed 119 canvasbacks from his sink box located off of Devil's Island. All of the other men named were also market hunters gunning out of their own batteries and most assuredly they made decoys the same as John Holly. It is more than reasonable to assume that these men began making decoys in the mid 1830's. At this same time that the business of killing ducks for the market was developing, sport gunning continued strongly, having been established some time ago on the rented points of land along the river shores closer to Baltimore. These clubs owned or rented grounds on the Bush and Gunpowder Rivers and one of the most famous and exclusive club locations was on Carroll's Island, lying at the mouth of the Gunpowder River. In 1849 this island had long been in the possession of a club of sportsmen headed by a wealthy Philadelphian and the members regularly gathered there to shoot wildfowl over decoys from the ambush blinds located in the coves and on the points of land jutting out into the water. Very early iron keeled decoys made by "Daddy" Holly and branded "Carroll's Island" are in several local collections and are among the earliest decoys used on the Upper Chesapeake Bay. They date from the period 1835-1840 and have seen service on the Flats for well over one hundred years.

Through the one hundred and forty odd years of development and use of the decoy on the Susquehanna Flats, two distinct styles of carving evolved, one in Harford County on the western shore of the Flats and the other, just across the river, in Cecil County on the eastern shore. Almost all of the carving in Harford County took place in one town, Havre de Grace, situated on the northwestern edge of the Flats, and the center of most of the activity in the market gunning era. In Cecil County the makers were spread through several small villages.

The two completely different styles that floated side by side around sink boxes all across the Flats should be referred to as the Havre de Grace school and the Cecil County school. The Havre de Grace decoys are characterized by a decoy body that almost always has an upswept tail near the top of the body, on diving ducks and marsh ducks, and no shelf on which the head and neck rest. The Cecil County birds, sometimes referred to as the Northeast River style by a few collectors, feature a tail usually straight and in the middle of the body and a shelf carving on which the head and neck are mounted. Of course there are exceptions on both sides of the river.

The originator of each of these styles remains obscured, but the decoys of John "Daddy" Holly of Havre de Grace and John B. Graham of Charlestown in Cecil County are fine early examples of each of the schools.

Just about every one of the decoys that were ever made for use on the Flats were solid. The few hollow decoys that are known show little difference in design from the solid birds. Many are made of white pine, but it is no secret that most makers would use any kind of wood available that could be worked. The heads were usually made of white pine, because it was abundant in earlier times, had a close grain, and was easily carved. Before the dams were constructed harnessing the power of the mighty Susquehanna River and hampering the free movement downstream, much of the wood used for decoy making was gathered from the river itself. When storms or springtime overflows wiped out bridges or flooded mill buildings or barns into the river from their too close to the water foundations, decoy makers down river were the recipients of the well seasoned white pine lumber that had been cut a century before.

On the earlier decoys made on the Flats, quite a bit of attention was given to detail carving around the bill and face area. Many of the makers carved nostrils and mandible separations on their bills and a few show nail carving on the end of the bill. A number of the makers impressed eyes into the wood with a .22 caliber shell casing or a similar sized object. Most eyes were painted on decoys from this region though, and a few used iron or copper upholstery tacks for eyes. I have never seen a Susquehanna Flats decoy with original glass eyes, although they were sometimes used farther down the Chesapeake Bay.

The only other noticeable extra carving on Flats decoys was the frequently used ridge down the middle of the back out to the end of the tail on marsh duck decoys. Both schools on each side of the river exhibited this characteristic and it is one instance where the tails on the Cecil County school of decoys are made near the top of the body rather than down in the middle.

A good deal of information has been written concerning the iron so called "horseshoe keels" that were used for ballast weight on the decoys in this area. The iron keels were actually no more than iron bars or rods that were heated and hammered into shape by the local blacksmiths. Only a few examined by this writer are actual horse shoes although, again, this was a common practice farther down the bay. Most of the decoys originally weighted with iron keels do predate 1900, but many decoys that were made before 1900 were originally ballasted with lead weights. Decoy makers learned early that they could easily cast their own style weights out of lead and even though some are of a similar design, each maker created a distinctively different weight. A little careful study will furnish much information on the identity of the maker. Very early Susquehanna Flats decoy men such as John Holly, Ben Dye, and John Graham cast their own lead weights that are unmistakably theirs and provide a great aid to the identification of their decoys.

The early method of attaching the anchor line to the decoy was through the means of a leather thong, a practice that was common all along the mid-Atlantic coast. Many older Flats decoys in original condition still retain their first leather thongs. Many others have lost theirs, to be replaced by the ring and staple, a later innovation. No one seems to be sure when the ring and staple came into general use, but it appears to have been after 1900, and has continued through till today.

The mooring anchors, for the most part, were conical or pyramidal in design to allow the weight to be pulled up easily through the grass without a lot of snagging. Many of the older ones were made of iron and were cast in the local foundries that were in operation in the area. These same foundries cast many tons of iron wing ducks for use as ballast on a sink box. Lead anchor weights came into general use later and were similar in shape to the iron weights that preceded them. Some iron anchors in the writer's collection are painted yellow, probably to simulate corn under the ducks during the years that the grass was scarce. The many different varieties of design in the anchor weights make for an interesting sidelight to one's decoy collection.

Decoys from the Susquehanna Flats in original paint are few and far between. A number of birds made by the Flats carvers for use in other areas are often found in original paint and these decoys, though not used on the Flats, are an important addition to a collection of decoys by the makers in this region. The primary reason for their importance is that so few birds that were hunted on the Flats are ever found with their first coat of paint. The decoys, as stated earlier in this book, were tools of the trade for the commercial hunter and anyone who works with tools knows that they must be properly maintained to be effective in the performance of their job. In the case of the market hunter's decoys it meant that the paint must be bright and fresh to attract the ducks, consequently they were painted at the beginning of each gunning season and sometimes once again during the season. Lots of these old decoys are found today with many coats of paint. Again, few are found with only one coat. Many fine collections of Susquehanna Flats decoys are built on decoys that have been repainted a number of times. This is not a desirable condition for decoys in collections from other areas, but an accepted fact if one wishes to collect birds made and used on the waters of the Flats.

Although the way the decoys were used and the fact that they were painted often would seem to dictate a simple paint style, this is not really the case. Many of the decoys, both hens and drakes, in canvasback, redhead, and blackhead, received some form of wing painting on the back. From earliest times through today the outlines of the wings and feathers within the wing outlines were painted on the birds. It was done more often on hens as opposed to drakes in the canvasbacks, but the sexes were embellished equally in the other species. Some of the wing, feather, and speculum painting is rather elaborate. Most of it is appealing to the collector's eye.

Early marsh duck decoys from the Flats are seldom found as few were made. But it appears that all of the major makers from this region made a few black duck decoys, and many of them made an occasional mallard, pintail, or teal. Some extremely fine marsh duck decoys are known. A number of the very early examples that I have seen exhibited feather painting very similar to the excellent Blair style from the Delaware River. The fact that Mr. John Blair owned a farm south of Elkton not far from the Flats, and that he was a contemporary of John Holly holds some fascination for this writer and bears further investigation. The scratch painting, which seems never to have been applied to the diving duck decoys, was practiced extensively here at an early date on the marsh species. It appears to have been initiated about 1890 by James T. Holly in Havre de Grace and was carried on in that town by Sam Barnes, Bob McGaw, Jim Currier, Madison Mitchell, and Paul Gibson. The technique has provided collectors with some very nicely done scratch painted black ducks. The result was effective and pleasing enough that it later lured Lem and Steve Ward of Crisfield, Maryland and Ira Hudson of Chincoteague, Virginia into trying it on their decoys.

The Susquehanna Flats is steeped in the history of waterfowl gunning in America and the decoy has played a major role throughout the years. It is significant that much of the earliest recorded history of duck shooting and decoys is centered around this body of water that was once one of the primary gathering areas of millions of wintering waterfowl, there to feed on the lush grasses that literally choked the waterways with the profusion of their growth; there too, to be enticed to the hunter's gun by their deceptive wooden counterpart that is so irresistible to decoy collectors today.

Upper left: Blue wing teal circa 1880 — Captain Ben Dye, Perryville, Maryland — original paint.

Upper right: Blue wing teal circa 1890 — George Washington Barnes, Carpenter's Point, Maryland — repainted as a hen scaup.

Middle left: Blue wing teal circa 1900 — Scott Jackson, Charlestown, Maryland — old repaint.

Middle right: Blue wing teal circa 1900 — Charles T. Wilson, Harve de Grace, Maryland — original paint.

Lower: Green wing teal circa 1890 — maker unknown, Havre de Grace, Maryland — old repaint.

Blue wing teal circa 1890 — maker unknown, Cecil County, Maryland — original paint. This decoy was possibly made by the "grand-daddy" of the Charlestown carvers, John B. Graham.

Blue wing teal circa 1880 — maker unknown, Susquehanna Flats, Maryland — original paint. A very well carved early teal decoy recently discovered. Note carved eyes.

Blue wing teal circa 1890 — James T. Holly, Havre de Grace, Maryland — original paint. An extremely fine and rare Upper Chesapeake Bay teal decoy. Of the type attributed, in previous publications, to Ben Holly, but later research and study indicate these decoys were made by James Holly.

Black duck circa 1890 — James T. Holly, Havre de Grace, Maryland — original paint. This decoy is a good example of the early scratch painting technique in the area.

Opposite page: above group starting "Upper left".

Upper left: Blue wing teal circa 1900 — Charles T. Wilson, Havre de Grace, Maryland — original paint. A rare Susquehanna Flats decoy painted in summer plumage.

Upper right: Blue wing teal, circa 1910 — John Wesley Williams, Port Deposit, Maryland — original paint — also painted in summer plumage.

Middle left: Mallard drake circa 1900 — James Holly, Havre de Grace, Maryland — original paint. A very rare decoy, only several are known.

Middle right: Black duck circa 1890 — James T. Holly, Havre de Grace, Maryland — original paint.

Lower left: Lesser scaup circa 1900 — John Holly, Jr., Havre de Grace, Maryland — old repaint — branded "SPESUTIE I. R. & G. CLUB".

Lower right: Green wing teal hen circa 1890 — James Holly, Havre de Grace, Maryland — original paint.

Upper: Two drake pintails circa 1890 — James T. Holly, Havre de Grace, Maryland — mostly original paint — extremely rare species of duck. Very few pintail decoys of this vintage are known from the Susquehanna Flats area.

Middle: Two black ducks circa 1890 — James T. Holly, Havre de Grace, Maryland — original paint. Black duck decoys of this quality from the Susquehanna Flats area are virtually non-existent in collections today.

Lower left: Lesser scaup circa 1890 — John "Daddy" Holly, Havre de Grace, Maryland — old Charlestown repaint. This is a late decoy by "Daddy" Holly and may have been made in conjunction with his sons.

Lower right: Redhead drake circa 1900 — James T. Holly, Havre de Grace, Maryland — original paint, branded "ELLIOTT" and on the other side of the weight branded "G.B.C." Made for use in North Carolina, the decoy has the normal Holly strip lead ballast unusually inletted into the bottom and fastened with square cut nails.

Upper left: Canvasback drake circa 1860 — John "Daddy" Holly, Havre de Grace, Maryland — old repaint. This decoy was formerly in the Reckless rig and is branded "RECKLESS" alongside its iron keel.

Upper right: Redhead drake circa 1890 — James T. Holly, Havre de Grace, Maryland — old repaint.

Middle: Canvasback hen circa 1890 — John "Daddy" Holly, Havre de Grace, Maryland — completely original paint, wing pattern painting, original tack eyes, original wooden keel. A rare and beautiful bird.

Lower left: Redhead drake circa 1875 — John "Daddy" Holly, Havre de Grace, Maryland — old worn original paint — branded "J.F.W."

Lower right: Drake scaup circa 1880 — James Holly, Havre de Grace, Maryland — old repaint — branded "F.S."

Upper left: Redhead drake circa 1890 — John "Daddy" Holly, Havre de Grace, Maryland — old repaint. Note impressed eyes and mandible carvings on the bill.

Upper right: Redhead drake circa 1880 — the Holly family, Havre de Grace, Maryland — old repaint. This decoy was made by either John Holly, Jr. or William Holly, and has a rectangular iron weight with the raised initials "T.J.H." inletted into the bottom.

Middle left: Canvasback drake circa 1880 — James T. Holly, Havre de Grace, Maryland — original paint — early style Holly body.

Middle right: Drake scaup circa 1910 — William Holly, Havre de Grace, Maryland — original paint. This decoy was hunted in North Carolina. Many Holly decoys have been found there.

Lower: Two drake scaup circa 1885 — possibly early "Daddy" Holly bodies with later Jim Holly heads, Havre de Grace, Maryland — old repaints — a bit different style but obviously by the Holly family.

Upper left: Lesser scaup hen circa 1885 — John "Daddy" Holly, Havre de Grace, Maryland — original paint — a very fine little decoy with the early style paint pattern.

Upper right: Scaup drake circa 1947 — Phil Kemp, Love Point, Maryland — original paint. Phil Kemp's decoys were all hand chopped with a hatchet.

Middle left: Scaup drake circa 1948 — Captain John Glen, Rock Hall, Maryland — original paint.

Middle right: Scaup drake circa 1929 — Robert F. McGaw, Havre de Grace, Maryland — original paint.

Lower left: Scaup drake circa 1968 — Captain Jesse Urie, Rock Hall, Maryland — original paint — one of the last full size decoys made by Captain Jesse.

Lower right: Scaup drake circa 1915 — Samuel T. Barnes, Havre de Grace, Maryland — original paint.

Upper left: Black duck circa 1900 — James Holly, Havre de Grace, Maryland — original paint — note the scratch painting.

Upper right: Black duck circa 1925 — Robert F. McGaw, Havre de Grace, Maryland — original paint — scratch painting.

Middle: Hen and drake mallards circa 1928 — Robert F. McGaw, Havre de Grace, Maryland — mint condition. These birds were never used for gunning decoys although they were made for that purpose. Starting in the mid-twenties, McGaw mounted some of his working decoys on these walnut bases and sold them for decorative purposes.

Lower left: Black duck circa 1930's — Ed Phillips, Cambridge, Maryland — original paint.

Lower right: Redhead drake circa 1885 — Captain Ben Dye, Perryville, Maryland — old repaint — complete bill carving is on this decoy.

Upper left: Black duck circa 1920 — Robert F. McGaw, Havre de Grace, Maryland — some original paint — snakey head style.

Upper right: Black duck circa 1900 — Robert F. McGaw, Havre de Grace, Maryland — original paint — hand chopped model.

Middle left: Scaup drake circa 1950 — Robert F. McGaw, Havre de Grace, Maryland — original paint — very late McGaw weighted by Gibson.

Middle right: Black duck circa 1930 — Robert F. McGaw, Havre de Grace, Maryland — original paint.

Lower left: Redhead drake circa 1935 — Robert F. McGaw, Havre de Grace, Maryland — original paint.

Lower right: Goldeneye drake circa 1935 — Robert F. McGaw, Havre de Grace, Maryland — original paint — one of only twelve made — very rare.

Upper left: Canvasback drake circa 1910 — Robert F. McGaw, Havre de Grace, Maryland — original paint — early, hand chopped style.

Upper right: Black duck circa 1925 — James Currier, Havre de Grace, Maryland — original paint.

Middle left: Baldpate drake circa 1939 — R. Madison Mitchell, Havre de Grace, Maryland — original paint.

Middle right: Baldpate drake circa 1949 — Paul Gibson, Havre de Grace, Maryland — original paint.

Lower left: Black duck circa 1940 — R. Madison Mitchell, Havre de Grace, Maryland — original paint.

Lower right: Mallard hen circa 1968 — Paul Gibson, Havre de Grace, Maryland — original paint.

Upper left: Mallard hen circa 1936 — R. Madison Mitchell, Havre de Grace, Maryland — original paint — a lovely bird in perfect original condition.

Upper right: Canvasback drake circa 1940 — R. Madison Mitchell, Havre de Grace, Maryland — original paint.

Middle: Black duck circa 1948 — R. Madison Mitchell, Havre de Grace, Maryland — original paint — slightly oversized — used on the Susquehanna River in Pennsylvania.

Lower left: Scaup hen circa 1941 — R. Madison Mitchell, Havre de Grace, Maryland — original paint.

Lower right: Redhead drake circa 1938 — R. Madison Mitchell, Havre de Grace, Maryland — original paint.

Upper: Drake and hen canvasback, circa 1940's — James Currier, Havre de Grace, Maryland — original paint.

Middle: Drake and hen scaup circa 1925 — James Currier, Havre de Grace, Maryland — original paint.

Lower left: Hen canvasback circa 1925 — James Currier, Havre de Grace, Maryland — original paint.

Lower right: Drake redhead circa 1940's — James Currier, Havre de Grace, Maryland — original paint.

Upper left: Canvasback drake circa 1920 — possibly James Currier, Havre de Grace, Maryland — old repaint.

Upper right: Canvasback drake circa 1920 — Carroll "Wally" Algard, Charlestown, Maryland — old repaint.

Middle: Canvasback drake circa 1930's — maker unknown, Susquehanna River, original paint.

Lower: Scaup drake circa 1890 — James T. Holly, Havre de Grace, Maryland — original paint — an extremely rare and finely carved wooden wing duck made to be used on a sink box frame.

Upper left: Canvasback drake circa 1870 — John B. Graham, Charlestown, Maryland — old repaint — branded "J. COUDON".

Upper right: Canvasback hen circa 1875 — John "Daddy" Holly, Havre de Grace, Maryland — some original paint. Branded "SUSQUEHANNA" which was the sister ship to the Reckless. There must have been the customary large rig of decoys on this scow, but strangely this is the only decoy so branded that has turned up.

Middle: Canvasback circa 1920 — Samuel T. Barnes, Havre de Grace, Maryland — original paint — a rare cork model by Sam Barnes.

Lower left: Canvasback drake circa 1915 — Scott Jackson, Charlestown, Maryland — old repaint.

Lower right: Canvasback drake circa 1920 — Joseph Dye, Havre de Grace, Maryland — old repaint.

Upper: Black duck circa 1890 — John B. Graham, Charlestown, Maryland — original paint. Note hollow three piece construction. This bird is one of the few hollow Susquehanna Flats decoys known.

Middle left: Black duck circa 1880 — John B. Graham, Charlestown, Maryland — old repaint.

Middle right: Canvasback drake circa 1875 — John B. Graham, Charlestown, Maryland — old repaint — an extremely rare and early sleeper made for use on the Susquehanna Flats, but discovered years later on Cobb Island, Virginia.

Lower left: Black duck circa 1900 — maker unknown — Susquehanna Flats — old repaint.

Lower right: Lesser scaup circa 1885 — maker unknown — Charlestown area — old repaint.

Opposite:

Upper left: Canvasback drake circa 1875 — Captain Ben Dye, Stumps Point, Maryland — decoy is repainted and was used as a black duck. Its diminutive size is noteworthy and was a characteristic typical of Ben Dye's work.

Upper right: Scaup drake circa 1880 — Captain Ben Dye, Perryville, Maryland — old repaint. This bird has finely detailed carving around the head and bill area. There are nostrils, mandibles, nail, and end of the bill carving that is sometimes found in Ben Dye's work.

Middle left: Redhead drake circa 1900 — Joseph Dye, Havre de Grace, Maryland — some original paint.

Middle right: Scaup drake circa 1910 — Joseph Dye, Havre de Grace, Maryland — completely original paint.

Lower left: Black duck circa 1900 — Taylor Boyd, Perryville, Maryland — old repaint. A rare decoy that exhibits the classy sleekness in most of Boyd's decoys. As is the case with most marsh duck decoys made in this area, there is a ridge running through the top of the tail.

Lower right: Redhead drake circa 1910 — Taylor Boyd, Perryville, Maryland — old repaint. All of Taylor Boyd's decoys had mandible carvings in the bill and a very definite square cut notch on each side where the tail joins the body.

Next page:

Upper left: Black duck circa 1910 — Joseph Dye, Havre de Grace, Maryland — old repaint. A fine rare decoy by the son of the famous Susquehanna Flats decoy maker, Captain Ben Dye.

Upper right: Black duck circa 1890 — Captain Ben Dye, Stumps Point, Perryville, Maryland — old repaint — a good example of the stylish flair of later decoys by Ben Dye.

Middle: Canvasback drake circa 1850, possibly earlier — Captain Ben Dye, Perryville, Maryland — some original paint showing — branded for and used later in the P. K. Barnes rig. This decoy says it all for classic Susquehanna Flats decoys. It's a canvasback, very early, beautiful in design, branded, and it has some original paint and the original ballast weight. A rare decoy.

Lower left: Scaup drake circa 1910 — Joseph Dye, Havre de Grace, Maryland — perfect original paint — as found condition.

Lower right: Blue wing teal circa 1880 — Captain Ben Dye, Perryville, Maryland — original paint.

Upper left: Canvasback drake circa 1880 — John B. Graham, Charlestown, Maryland — old repaint.

Upper right: Canvasback drake circa 1880 — John B. Graham, Charlestown, Maryland — old repaint.

Middle: Drake and hen canvasback circa 1920 — Henry Lockard, Elk Neck, Maryland — old repaint by Bob McGaw.

Lower: Drake and hen canvasback circa 1925 — maker unknown, Havre de Grace, Maryland — drake repainted, hen original paint.

Upper left: Canvasback drake circa 1930 — Taylor Boyd, Perryville, Maryland — old repaint.

Upper right: Canvasback drake circa 1925 — Carroll "Wally" Algard, Charlestown, Maryland — old repaint.

Middle left: Canvasback drake circa 1890 — maker unknown, Havre de Grace, Maryland — old repaint.

Middle right: Canvasback drake circa 1900 — Samuel T. Barnes, Havre de Grace, Maryland — old repaint — branded "J.D. Poplar" in bottom.

Lower: Scaup drake circa 1885 — James T. Holly, Havre de Grace, Maryland — old repaint.

Upper left: Black duck circa 1910 — Leonard Pryor, Chesapeake City, Maryland — original paint — hollow, two piece construction. Note raised wing tips similar to Delaware River style.

Upper right: Pintail drake circa 1915 — Leonard Pryor, Chesapeake City, Maryland — original paint — hollow, two piece construction — impressed eyes as in preceding black duck.

Middle left: Canvasback drake circa 1920 — Leonard Pryor, Chesapeake City, Maryland — original paint. Pryor's canvasback is similar in style to his two preceding birds, but solid. All Pryor birds had nostril carving.

Middle right: Canvasback drake circa 1920 — Leonard Pryor, Chesapeake City, Maryland — old repaint — one of the few makers who made sleepers on the Susquehanna Flats.

Lower: Hen and drake canvasback circa 1950's — Milton Watson, Chesapeake City, Maryland — original paint — high head tollers.

Upper left: Drake canvasback circa 1910 — Scott Jackson, Charlestown, Maryland — old repaint.

Upper right: Drake canvasback circa 1932 — Bob Litzenberg, Elkton, Maryland — original paint.

Lower: Hen and drake redhead circa 1931 — Bob Litzenberg, Elkton, Maryland — original paint.

Upper: Black duck circa 1890 — William Heverin, Charlestown, Maryland — original paint.

Middle: Canvasback drake circa 1900 — William Heverin, Charlestown, Maryland — old repaint. An original wooden keel with a good sized chunk of lead is attached to compensate for the extremely high head of this toller decoy. These long necked decoys by Heverin are few and far between.

Lower left: Canvasback drake circa 1885 — William Heverin, Charlestown, Maryland — old repaint. A very small canvasback decoy that exemplifies the stories that Heverin would make his decoys out of whatever size piece of wood that he had on hand.

Lower right: Canvasback hen circa 1935 — William Heverin, Charlestown, Maryland — original paint. Formerly in the rig of Lou Pennock of Greenbank, Maryland, and branded "L. Pennock" in the bottom.

Upper: Two black ducks circa 1920 — William Heverin, Charlestown, Maryland — left bird in original paint, right bird in old repaint. Photo shows two completely different style black ducks by Heverin.

Middle left: Drake scaup circa 1935 — William Heverin, Charlestown, Maryland — original paint. Note Charlestown wing pattern.

Middle right: Hen canvasback circa 1925 — William Heverin, Charlestown, Maryland — original paint. Heverin painted the wing pattern on the hen canvasback only.

Lower: Drake and hen redhead circa 1935 — William Heverin, Charlestown, Maryland — original paint.

Upper left: Black duck circa 1952 — Captain Jesse Urie, Rock Hall, Maryland — original paint.

Upper right: Drake scaup circa 1948 — August Heinefield, Rock Hall, Maryland — original paint. All Rock Hall area decoys have to have unpainted ballast weights to be in original paint.

Middle left: Redhead drake circa 1910 — Charles Nelson Barnard, Havre de Grace, Maryland — original paint — one of the rare hollow decoys from the Susquehanna Flats area.

Middle right: Canvasback drake circa 1890 — Joseph Dye, Havre de Grace, Maryland — old repaint. Note the long paddle tail and the snakey head — a fantastic and beautiful form.

Lower left: Canvasback drake circa 1880 — John B. Graham, Charlestown, Maryland — old repaint. The design here shows a strong similarity to the "Cleveland canvasbacks" — supporting my opinion that John Graham made these canvasbacks.

Lower right: Redhead drake circa 1952 — Henry Lockard, Elk Neck, Maryland — old repaint by Severin Hall.

Upper: Black duck circa 1890 — William Heverin, Charlestown, Maryland — original paint.

Middle left: Canvasback drake circa 1922 — Columbus "Lum" Fletcher, Havre de Grace, Maryland — old repaint. Lum Fletcher was one of the few Havre de Grace makers with a raised shelf carving on which the head and neck rest. He almost always carved nostrils and mandibles in his bills. Branded "G.A.E." on bottom.

Middle right: Canvasback drake circa 1935 — Al Thomas, Swan Creek, Aberdeen, Maryland — original paint. The decoys of this man are often referred to as "shoe bills" because the underside of his bills remind one of the outline of a shoe.

Lower: Black duck circa 1917 — Leonard Pryor, Chesapeake City, Maryland — original paint — raised wing carving — impressed eyes, and solid body.

Upper left: Black duck circa 1955 — Captain Jesse Urie, Rock Hall, Maryland — original paint.

Upper right: Black duck circa 1915 — Samuel T. Barnes, Havre de Grace, Maryland — original paint — scarce cork black duck by Sam Barnes. He is known to have made Canada geese, canvasback, scaup, redhead, and black ducks out of cork.

Middle: Black duck circa 1950 — Captain Jesse Urie, Rock Hall, Maryland — original paint — oversized model. Captain Urie made only black ducks and canvasbacks in the oversized model.

Lower: Black duck circa 1890 — Samuel T. Barnes, Havre de Grace, Maryland — old repaint. The only wooden black duck decoy by Sam Barnes known in a collection today.

Upper: Redhead hen circa 1890 — Samuel T. Barnes, Havre de Grace, Maryland — mostly original paint.

Middle: Canvasback drake circa 1929 — Henry Lockard, Elk Neck, Maryland — old repaint by Bob McGaw of Havre de Grace, Maryland.

Lower: Canvasback hen circa 1910 — Samuel T. Barnes, Havre de Grace, Maryland — old repaint.

Upper left: Drake scaup circa 1870 — John B. Graham, Charlestown, Maryland — old repaint.

Upper right: Black duck circa 1880 — John B. Graham, Charlestown, Maryland — old repaint.

Middle left: Redhead drake circa 1885 — John B. Graham, Charlestown, Maryland — old repaint.

Middle right: Canvasback drake circa 1875 — John B. Graham, Charlestown, Maryland — old repaint.

Lower left: Redhead drake circa 1870 — John B. Graham, Charlestown, Maryland — original paint — branded "R. M. VANDIVER".

Lower right: Canvasback drake circa 1880 — John B. Graham, Charlestown, Maryland — old repaint — very rare wooden wing duck.

The selection of decoys in this plate illustrate clearly the many different styles of John B. Graham.

Two iron wing ducks, one canvasback, one redhead, circa 1890 — made on the pattern of John B. Graham, Charlestown, Maryland. These iron wing decoys were used as ballast on a sink box to keep the device sunk to the proper depth.

Canvasback hen, circa 1890 — maker unknown, Perryville, Maryland — original paint — made to be used as a wooden wing duck.

Upper: Canada goose circa 1950 — R. Madison Mitchell, Havre de Grace, Maryland — original paint. A hole has been drilled on each side of the ballast weight, indicating use as a field decoy.

Middle: Canada goose circa 1910 — William Holly, Havre de Grace, Maryland — old repaint. One of the earlier goose decoys made in Havre de Grace.

Lower: Canada goose circa 1969 — Paul Gibson, Havre de Grace, Maryland — original paint.

Upper — left to right: Canvasback drake — Wally Algard, canvasback drake — Ron Rue, two Canada geese — Robert F. McGaw, two Canada geese — maker unknown.

Lower — left to right: Mallard drake — Miles Hancock, mallard drake — Captain Jesse Urie, two Canada geese and a canvasback drake — maker unknown, scaup drake — Miles Hancock.

Upper — left to right: Canada goose — Ron Rue, baldpate drake — Ron Rue, canvasback drake — Robert F. McGaw, Canada goose — Milton Watson, canvasback drake — maker unknown, flying mallard drake — maker unknown.

Lower — left to right: Hen and drake canvasback — Milton Watson, two drakes, one hen canvasback — Captain John Glen, red breasted merganser drake — Miles Hancock, canada goose — John McKenny.

Upper — Canvasback drake circa 1925 — maker unknown, Susquehanna River, Pennsylvania — old repaint.

Lower: Drake and hen redhead circa 1945 — Robert Sellers, Silver Spring, Pennsylvania — original paint.

Drake green wing teal circa 1880 — Edward Cabot, Principio, Maryland — Susquehanna River — original paint. Head joined to body with a dovetail joint. Extremely
hollow and light. Made by a talented person, most probably a cabinetmaker. Obviously by the same maker of the Canada goose decoy in the frontis portrait in
Adele Earnest's book.

Drake canvasback circa 1900 — maker unknown, Susquehanna River, Pennsylvania — old working paint. A dandy little decoy, short and round, exhibiting characteristics of "up the river" makers, but more finely done than most.

Coot circa 1960's — Jim Pierce, Havre de Grace, Maryland — original paint. A nice example of a contemporary working decoy.

Canvasback hen circa 1910 — Charles Nelson Barnard, Havre de Grace, Maryland — original paint. This classic Susquehanna Flats decoy has everything most any collector could ask for: an extremely high head, the rare hen bird, original paint, age, and a brand — "J. PUSEY" — in the bottom.

Canvasback hen circa 1915 — Samuel T. Barnes, Havre de Grace, Maryland — original paint.

Canvasback drake circa 1850 — Captain Ben Dye, Perryville, Maryland — traces of original paint. An exceptional decoy, possibly the earliest in the author's collection.

J.J. Audubon, engraving of Canvas Backed Duck, courtesy The Old Print Shop, New York City.

Black duck circa 1915 — Leonard Pryor, Chesapeake City, Maryland — original paint. A lovely hollow decoy, very Delaware River in style with its raised wing tip carving and feathering detail paint.

Black duck circa 1910 — William Heverin, Charlestown, Maryland — mostly original paint. An extremely long, high tail model Heverin black duck. A rare and desirable species by Heverin.

Goldeneye drake circa 1890 — maker unknown, Susquehanna River in Pennsylvania. Traces of original paint — found in the Columbia, Pennsylvania area — this decoy has a chestnut head and a body of cherry.

Canada goose, circa 1968 — Paul Gibson, Havre de Grace, Maryland — original paint — unusual preener.

Canada goose, circa 1915 — Samuel T. Barnes, Havre de Grace, Maryland — old repaint. Rare cork decoy.

Coot circa 1947 — Severn Hall, Northeast Maryland — original paint. Severn Hall made cork coot and canvasback decoys in the 1940's for use on the Susquehanna Flats.

Drake scaup circa 1925 — Robert F. McGaw, Havre de Grace, Maryland — mint condition.   McGaw's working decoy mounted on an ornamental walnut stand by McGaw in 1925.

Redhead wooden patterns for use in casting iron sink box decoys — circa 1890. Front one by Ben Dye, Perryville, Maryland, and rear one by his son Joe Dye, Havre de Grace, Maryland. Both formerly in the Mackey collection.

Scaup drake circa 1910 — Joseph Dye, Havre de Grace, Maryland — original paint — another typical undersize Susquehanna Flats blackhead.

Canvasback drake circa 1880 — the so called "Cleveland canvasback" — Charlestown, Maryland — old repaint. Much ado is made over these decoys, for what reason one wonders. The strong similarities between them and many of John Graham's birds seem to indicate that he made them.

Drake canvasback circa 1900 — George W. Barnes, Carpenter's Point, Maryland — original paint, near mint condition. This decoy was used very little, if at all.

Black duck circa 1880 — George Washington Barnes, Carpenter's Point, Maryland — original paint. The feeding or swimming head position makes this bird a very different and important addition to the decoy history of the Susquehanna Flats. It was found in with a bushwhack rig of canvasbacks, and was used as a "John duck" for the anchor.

Ruddy duck circa 1890 — maker unknown, Cecil County, Maryland — a rare early Upper Bay ruddy duck decoy — old repaint.

Canvasback hen circa 1880 — John "Daddy" Holly, Havre de Grace, Maryland — original paint. Decoys from the Susquehanna Flats, of this period and in original paint, are seldom found.

Drake canvasback circa 1900 — James T. Holly, Havre de Grace, Maryland — original paint. This decoy was used on the Susquehanna River in Pennsylvania and its fine original condition can be partly attributed to its use in fresh water.

Hen and drake pintail circa 1936 — R. Madison Mitchell, Havre de Grace, Maryland — original paint. Probably as fine and as early a pair of pintails ever made by Madison.

Drake redhead circa 1900 — James T. Holly, Havre de Grace, Maryland — original paint — used in North Carolina, has the typical Holly strip lead weight inletted flush into the bottom.

Top Decoy Counter-clockwise:

Drake Pintail — Lloyd Sterling — C-1920 — Crisfield, Maryland — Original paint.

Drake Pintail — Lem and Steve Ward — C-1936 — Crisfield, Maryland — Original paint.

Drake Baldpate — Lem and Steve Ward — C-1930 — Crisfield, Maryland — Repainted by Lem.

Drake Pintail — Lloyd Tyler — C-1925 — Crisfield, Maryland — Original paint.

Top Two Decoys Clockwise

    Drake and Hen Mallard — Lem and Steve Ward — C-1948 — Crisfield, Maryland — Original paint.

    Hen Scaup — The Ward Brothers — C-1948 — Crisfield, Maryland — Original paint.

    Drake Redhead — The Ward Brothers — C-1948 — Crisfield, Maryland — Original paint.

    Drake Goldeneye — The Ward Brothers — C-1948 — Crisfield, Maryland — Original paint.

    Hen Goldeneye — The Ward Brothers — C-1948 — Crisfield, Maryland — Original paint.

    Hen Redhead — The Ward Brothers — C-1948 — Crisfield, Maryland — Original paint.

    Drake Scaup — The Ward Brothers — C-1948 — Crisfield, Maryland — Original paint.

Middle Decoy

    Hen Canvasback — The Ward Brothers — C-1948 — Crisfield, Maryland — Original paint.

Drake canvasback circa 1915 — Thomas Barnard, Havre de Grace, Maryland — old repaint — very large oversized can decoy by the brother of C. N. Barnard.

Drake canvasback circa 1910 — Henry Lockard, Elk Neck, Maryland — nice old repaint by Jim Currier. A beautiful, high headed Lockard can.

Drake canvasback circa 1905 — Carroll Cleveland Algard, Charlestown, Maryland — old repaint. An early, remarkably fine canvasback decoy by "Wally" Algard.

John B. Graham C-1880

Top Decoy Clockwise

Canada Goose — Edson Gray — C-1925 — Ocean View, Delaware — Original paint.

Brant — Ira Hudson — C-1910 — Chincoteague, Virginia — Original paint.

Drake Canvasback — Ira Hudson — C-1910 — Chincoteague, Virginia — Original paint.

Drake Baldpate — Lem and Steve Ward — 1948 — Crisfield, Maryland — Original paint.

Black Duck — James T. Holly — C-1890 — Havre de Grace, Maryland — Original paint.

Drake Canvasback — Lem and Steve Ward — C-1946 — Crisfield, Maryland — Original paint.

Brant — The Cobb Family — C-1890 — Cobb Island, Virginia — Original paint.

Middle Two Decoys

Top: Drake Canvasback — Capt. Ben Dye — C-1850 — Perryville, Maryland — Old repaint.

Bottom: Drake Goldeneye — Robert F. McGaw — C-1935 — Havre de Grace, Maryland — Original paint.

Top Decoy Clockwise

Drake Pintail — James T. Holly — C-1890 — Havre de Grace, Maryland — Mostly original paint.

Drake Mallard — James T. Holly — C-1890 — Havre de Grace, Maryland — Original paint.

Hen Canvasback — Samuel T. Barnes — C-1900 — Havre de Grace, Maryland — Original paint.

Drake Canvasback — James T. Holly — C-1900 — Havre de Grace, Maryland — Original paint.

Drake Redhead — James T. Holly — C-1900 — Havre de Grace, Maryland — Original paint.

Hen Mallard — Madison Mitchell — C-1936 — Havre de Grace, Maryland — Original paint.

Black Duck — James T. Holly — C-1890 — Havre de Grace, Maryland — Original paint.

Three Birds in the Middle from Top Clockwise

Drake Canvasback — C-1850 — Capt. Ben Dye — Perryville, Maryland — Old paint.

Drake Goldeneye — Robert F. McGaw — C-1935 — Havre de Grace, Maryland — Original paint.

Hen Canvasback — Henry Davis — C-1890 — Perryville, Maryland — Original paint.

Canada goose circa 1920's — Paul Gibson, Havre de Grace, Maryland — original paint. An early goose decoy made by Gibson before he began to use a lathe to turn up his birds.

Canada goose and black duck folding racks circa 1920's — Joseph Coudon, Aiken, Maryland — mint original condition. Unusual decoys manufactured near the Flats and shipped all over the country. Forerunners of very similar rack decoys used on the Susquehanna Flats today.

CHAPTER 5

Chesapeake Bay

> The Chesapeake Bay, with its
> tributary streams, has, from its
> discovery, been known as the
> greatest resort of waterfowl in
> the United States.
>
> Dr. J. J. Sharpless
> *Cabinet of Natural History, 1830*

The statement above, made over 100 years ago, would evoke arguments from many waterfowling regions in the United States today. Sad to say, the arguments would be raised from strong ground. The Chesapeake Bay, a magnificent body of water once unequalled in this country for its richness, has fallen somewhat to poorer times. Years of neglect and abuse have only in recent years begun to subside and their negative results reversed. Whether or not the Chesapeake can ever return to its time of former opulence, a time when the waters were replete with fish and the marshes and creeks host to the staggering numbers of wintering wildfowl, only time can tell.

Once the luxuriant grasses were so thick it was nearly impossible to wade through them dipping the abundant hard crabs, and there wasn't a day during the summer, on the right tide, that one couldn't return to their pier with a dozen succulent soft shells, an epicurean's delight.

L.T. Ward and Bro., circa 1948.

Top: Hen and Drake Red Breasted Merganser — Harry V. Shourds — C-1890 — Tuckerton, New Jersey — Original paint.

2nd Level: Drake and Hen Mallard — Nathan Rowley Horner — C-1930 — West Creek, New Jersey — Original paint.

3rd Level, Left: Drake Redhead — Harry V. Shourds — C-1890 — Tuckerton, New Jersey — Original paint.

3rd Level, Right: Drake Bufflehead — Harry V. Shourds — C-1890 — Tuckerton, New Jersey — Original paint.

Bottom: Drake and Hen Red Breasted Merganser — Lloyd Parker — C-1900 — Parkertown, New Jersey — Original paint.

Top: Drake and Hen Green Wing Teal — Lem and Steve Ward — C-1948 — Crisfield, Maryland — Original paint.

2nd Level, Right: Blue Wing Teal — Maker unknown — C-1890 — Susquehanna Flats — Original paint.

2nd Level, Left: Blue Wing Teal — James T. Holly — C-1890 — Havre de Grace, Maryland — Original paint.

3rd Level: Hen and Drake Blue Wing Teal — Reginald Marter — C-1950 — Delanco, New Jersey — Original paint.

Bottom Right: Drake Blue Wing Teal — Blair School — C-1890 — Delaware River — Original paint.

Bottom Left: Drake Green Wing Teal — Blair School — C-1890 — Delaware River — Original paint.

With autumn's arrival came the season of oysters and waterfowl. The dredge boats, our beloved skipjacks, under full sail over the bars foretold of coming fried oyster suppers at the local firehouse. And the fowl! The myriads of winged denizens from the north country here to winter on the lush vegetable beds of the Chesapeake. What could be finer than a brace of plump cans, fattened on wild celery from the Flats that were drawn too close over the decoys to the hunter's gun at Eastern Neck Island, or lured within range at Cook's Point, and later that evening were reposing in roasted splendor on candlelit tables in farmhouses everywhere.

Duck shooting was popular throughout the tidewater country of the Chesapeake and decoys were made in practically every area near the water. Names like Rock Hall, Kent Island, Tilghman, Hooper's Island, and Crisfield were important centers of decoy making.

The Rock Hall school was handled ably by men like Captain John Glen, August Heinefield, and Captain Jess Urie. Their decoys resembled somewhat the decoys of Havre de Grace, but the boat building influence of John Glen was very evident in their earlier style. Decoys for nearly every species of duck and Canada goose were made by these three gentlemen in the waterfront fishing town of Rock Hall from the 1920's through the 1960's. An era ended when Captain Jesse passed away recently at the age of 78.

From Love Point on the northern tip of Kent Island on down the Chesapeake Bay to the lower island of Hooper's Island a vast and intricate stretch of waterways greet the migrating waterfowl as they extend their visit into the mid-bay region. The decoy makers who lived in the picturesque villages that were built by the seventeenth century English settlers on the shores of these rivers and creeks inherited the independence of their ancestors and it surfaced in the individuality of design in the decoys they carved.

The names of some of the towns, Cambridge, Tilghman, Oxford, Stevensville, Easton, and Hoopersville, are strong evidence of the English heritage, while others such as Romancoke, Choptank, Nanticoke, and Fishing Creek bring to mind the legacy of the first settlers in this territory. A life on the water, in which gunning played a big role, was the lot of most of the men in these communities. Their decoys were as important and basic to them as their work boats, and there were few of these watermen who didn't try their hand at whittling their own decoys. On this section of the Chesapeake all of the decoys were hand made. They were first roughed to shape by hatchet, then worked down with a drawknife or spokeshave and finished by hand sanding. The painting was usually done quickly in a simple, but effective pattern. It captured the basic colors of the bird and little else. Finding a decoy from the mid-bay area in original paint is seldom accomplished and when one is collected, the discoverer may search for a long time to find its mate in like condition. The fairly heavy salt water works hard on the commonly used house paint and it does not hold up for very long before a new coat of paint is needed.

The decoys in this region were ballasted with every sort of anything that would do the job and was handy. Many items found on or around boats were commonly used and it was not unusual to see an oar lock seat, a scupper, or a tie down on the bottom of a decoy. An old rusty bolt, a piece of horseshoe or a piece of a plow were also often used. A sometimes average decoy from this section becomes vastly more interesting when the decoy is turned over and the weight is found to be some out-of-the-ordinary ballast.

Farther down the Chesapeake near the lower end of the bay in Maryland, one comes to Crisfield, the home of the far famed Lem and Steve Ward, and here, as has been said before, all sameness of the decoys of the Chesapeake Bay disappears.

Lem and Steve Ward made some of the finest and most artistic working decoys that were ever created to deceive wildfowl into thinking they were putting in among their brethren. There has never been any doubt as to the genius displayed by these two fine gentlemen when it came to their making of "wildfowl counterfeits." The exquisite painting, the realistic attitude, and the unquestioned conformation of their birds is, in the opinion of most collectors, unsurpassed in the decoy collecting world of today.

The Ward Bros. developed and refined the Crisfield school of decoys that had been started around the turn of the century by their father, L. Travis Ward, Sr., and the Sterling Family. The members of the Sterling Family, "Gunner" Will and Noah among them, produced decoys similar in style to the Ward's, but lacking the fineness so apparent in Lem and Steve's work. The names of Tyler, Nelson, Dize, and Lawson are usually mentioned in the same breath with Crisfield decoys. These family names, all notable in the decoy making history of this century, also figured prominently in the settlement of the town of Crisfield.

When one thinks of Crisfield decoys, flat bottomed birds, wide at the hips and narrow breasted, come to mind. Almost all were made solid and slightly over-sized, because a lot of the hunting in the Tangier Sound area is done on big open water.

Crisfield is an out of the way, nineteenth century town built on the Chesapeake Bay seafood industry. It has been famous from the beginning for its crabs, oysters, and fish, but the waterfowl shooting available there has always been equally famous; and when Crisfield is mentioned today, often the Ward Bros. and their duck decoys become the topic of conversation.

The information contained so far in this introduction to the Chesapeake Bay and its decoys has been concerned solely with the Eastern Shore of Maryland. This is not intended as a slight on the Western Shore. Duck hunting has always been and still is a popular pastime on this side of the Bay, but a scant few makers of decoys from the Western Shore are known. This includes the entire section from just south of the Susquehanna Flats all the way down to the Potomac River. Some of the rivers that empty into this side of the bay are rich in early duck shooting lore, particularly those just north of Baltimore. Millers Island, which lies at the mouth of Back River, is known to have been a ducking ground of some repute and of course the Gunpowder, Bush, and Middle River sections have previously been referred to in this book. Many or perhaps most of the decoys used in these areas were made by the makers in Havre de Grace and other towns on the Flats. It was just a short boat ride north and in 1890 decoys were selling in Havre de Grace for just twenty cents each.

Opposite page:

Top Right: Hen Canvasback — John Dawson — C-1930 — Trenton, New Jersey — Original paint.

Top Left: Hen Merganser — John Dawson — C-1930 — Trenton, New Jersey — Original paint.

Middle Right: Drake Pintail — John Dawson — C-1930 — Trenton, New Jersey — Original paint.

Middle Left: Drake Pintail — John Blair — C-1870 — Philadelphia, Pennsylvania — Original paint.

4th Row, Right: Baldpate Drake — Robert F. McGaw — C-1935 — Havre de Grace, Maryland — Original paint.

4th Row, Left: Baldpate Drake — Maker and date unknown — New Jersey Coast — Original paint.

Bottom, Left: Redhead Drake — John Dawson — C-1930 — Trenton, New Jersey — Original paint.

Bottom, Right: Black Duck — Dan English — C-1920 — Florence, New Jersey — Original paint.

Below:

Top Decoy Clockwise

     Brant — The Cobb Family — C-1890 — Cobb Island, Virginia — Original paint.

     Brant — Dave Watson — C-1900 — Chincoteague, Virginia — Original paint.

     Drake Canvasback — Ira Hudson — C-1930 — Chincoteague, Virginia — Mint original condition.

     Black Duck — Ronald Rue — Cambridge, Maryland — Original paint.

     Drake Canvasback — Ira Hudson — C-1910 — Chincoteague, Virginia — Original paint.

     Brant — Ira Hudson — C-1910 — Chincoteague, Virginia — Original paint.

Bird in Center

     Drake Canvasback — Ira Hudson — C-1930 — Chincoteague, Virginia — Mint original paint and condition.

One later decoy maker who still turns out a fine decoy lives at Wilson Point on Middle River. His name is Charles Bryan and he learned his trade under "Speed" Joiner of Betterton, Maryland, almost directly across the Bay. Another maker from Baltimore, Maryland was Mr. Al Bell who made duck and goose decoys and a few swan. Little is known of this maker at the time of this writing, but maybe someone will come forward with information and a few of his decoys when they read this book.

South of Baltimore, from the waters of the Magothy, Severn, South, West, and Patuxent Rivers, we find no decoy makers. Many of the decoys that turn up here come from across the bay and they were apparently easy enough and inexpensive enough to obtain, that the duck shooters here felt no need to make their own. Again, perhaps, after reading this book, someone will come forward with needed history at a later date.

The Chesapeake Bay decoys are of varied styles and patterns and were designed by the many makers that lived along its shores. They were once plentiful on these waters during the winter months, but most have now been retired and are stacked away in dark corners, their owners hoping that one day the ducks will return and the services of the silent wooden stool will once again be needed.

Pair of mallards circa 1950 — T. Gilbert Lowe, Baltimore, Maryland — hollow with original paint.

Drake canvasback circa 1950 — Charles Joiner, Betterton, Maryland — original paint — from the rig of the author of *Gunning the Chesapeake,* the late Mr. Roy Walsh.

Upper: Two redhead drakes circa 1940's — August Heinefield, Rock Hall, Maryland — old repaint. Note high unswept tail.

Lower: Black duck, circa 1930 — Captain John Glen, Rock Hall, Maryland — old repaint.

Upper left: Black duck circa 1885 — John B. Graham, Charlestown, Maryland — old repaint.

Upper right: Black duck circa 1930 — Walter Bush, Newark, New Jersey — original paint.

Middle left: Black duck circa 1930's — John Vickers, Cambridge, Maryland — original paint.

Middle right: Black duck circa 1950 — Captain Jesse Urie, Rock Hall, Maryland — original paint.

Lower left: Black duck circa 1940 — Captain John Glen, Rock Hall, Maryland — original paint.

Lower right: Black duck circa 1956 — August Heinefield, Rock Hall, Maryland — original paint.

Upper left: Drake lesser scaup, circa 1940's — Charles Joiner, Betterton, Maryland — original paint.

Upper right: Drake canvasback circa 1940's — Charles Joiner, Betterton, Maryland — original paint — Ed Robinson rig.

Middle: Hen and drake mallard, circa 1950 — Charles Bryan, Wilson Point, Maryland — original paint.

Lower left: Mallard drake, circa 1955 — R. Madison Mitchell, Havre de Grace, Maryland — original paint.

Lower right: Baldpate drake circa 1955 — Captain Harry Jobes, Aberdeen, Maryland — original paint.

Canada goose circa 1930 — Edson Gray, Ocean View, Delaware — original paint — typical, oversized balsa working decoy by Mr. Gray, the only maker of note in Delaware.

Drake canvasback circa 1920's — maker unknown, Talbot County, Maryland — old worn and chipped original paint. This decoy was made in the Neavitt-Bozman area of Talbot County.

Upper: Drake and hen canvasback circa 1930 — Edson Gray, Ocean View, Delaware — original paint — solid.

Middle: Black duck circa 1925 — Edson Gray, Ocean View, Delaware — original paint — hollow carved.

Lower: Drake and hen scaup circa 1935 — Edson Gray, Ocean View, Delaware — original paint — solid.

Upper: Scaup drake circa 1950's — Elliott Bros., Easton, Maryland — original paint. Formerly in the Roy Walsh rig.

Middle: Canvasback drake, circa 1930 — Captain Ed Parsons, Oxford, Maryland — old repaint by the Elliot Bros.

Lower: Black duck circa 1930's — Edmund Hardcastle, Talbot County, Maryland — original paint.

White wing scoter, circa 1960's — Ron Rue, Cambridge, Maryland — original paint. An exceptionally fine hollow pine decoy, one of twelve made for hunting sea ducks near the mouth of the Choptank River.

Below, J.J. Audubon, engraving of Black or Surf Duck, courtesy The Old Print Shop, New York City.

Upper: Herring gull circa 1968 — Ron Rue, Cambridge, Maryland — original paint. Formerly in the rig of the Castle Haven Gun Club.

Middle: Hen and drake canvasback circa 1970 — Ron Rue, Cambridge, Maryland — original paint.

Lower left: Drake scaup circa 1970 — Ron Rue, Cambridge, Maryland — original paint.

Lower right: Laughing gull circa 1968 — Ron Rue, Cambridge, Maryland — original paint.

Drake scaup circa 1900 — maker unknown, South Dorchester County, Maryland — original paint. An attractive little unknown blackhead that is a little nicer than most decoys from this area.

Scaup drake circa 1930's — Ed Phillips, Cambridge, Maryland — original paint. A beautiful little decoy by one of the premier Dorchester County makers.

Drake and hen bufflehead circa 1950 — "Gunner" Alvin Meekins, Hoopers Island, Dorchester County, Maryland — original paint. Small tack eye "butterballs" of the type found throughout South Dorchester.

Flying red breasted merganser, circa 1950's — "Gunner" Alvin Meekins, Hoopers Island, Maryland — original paint. The only Chesapeake Bay flying decoy known.

Drake scaup circa 1940 — Captain Josiah Travers, Vienna, Maryland — original paint. A little known species by one of Dorchester County's better makers.

Drake and hen red breasted merganser circa 1950's — "Gunner" Alvin Meekins, Hooper's Island, Maryland — original paint. Examples of "fence post pheasants".

Upper: Three scaup drakes circa 1890 — makers unknown, Dorchester County, Maryland — original paint. All three decoys were made and used in the South Dorchester marshes referred to locally as "down below". All have original tack eyes and the bird in the middle is hollow with a half inch bottom board attached.

Middle: Ruddy duck circa 1910 — maker unknown, Dorchester County, Maryland — mostly original paint. The decoy fills most of Bill Mackey's requirements for it to be a ruddy duck. It is as wide as it is long, has a broad bill, a fat head, and white cheek patches.

Lower: Drake and hen scaup circa 1915 — maker unknown, Talbot County, Maryland — perfect original paint. The decoys have small blacksmith made iron keels in their bottoms.

Upper left: Hooded merganser drake circa 1940's — Judson Budd, Chincoteague, Virginia — original paint.

Upper right: Red breasted merganser drake circa 1950 — Clarence Hix "Pap" Creighton, Hoopers Island, Dorchester County, Maryland — original paint.

Middle: Red breasted merganser hen circa 1960's — "Gunner" Alvin Meekins, Hoopers Island, Dorchester County, Maryland — original paint.

Lower: Red breasted merganser drake circa 1960's — "Gunner" Alvin Meekins, Hoopers Island, Dorchester County, Maryland — original paint. Note pieces of chain for ballast weight, a typical Dorchester County characteristic.

Upper: Canada goose circa 1940's — Captain Josiah Travers, Vienna, Maryland — original paint — very interesting cork goose from Dorchester County. Head is attached to a screen door spring through the body so the head would impart a rocking movement when rigged out on the water.

Lower: Black duck circa 1940's — Captain Josiah Travers, Vienna, Maryland — original paint — original tack eyes in both this and the preceding goose decoy. One-inch bottom board is attached.

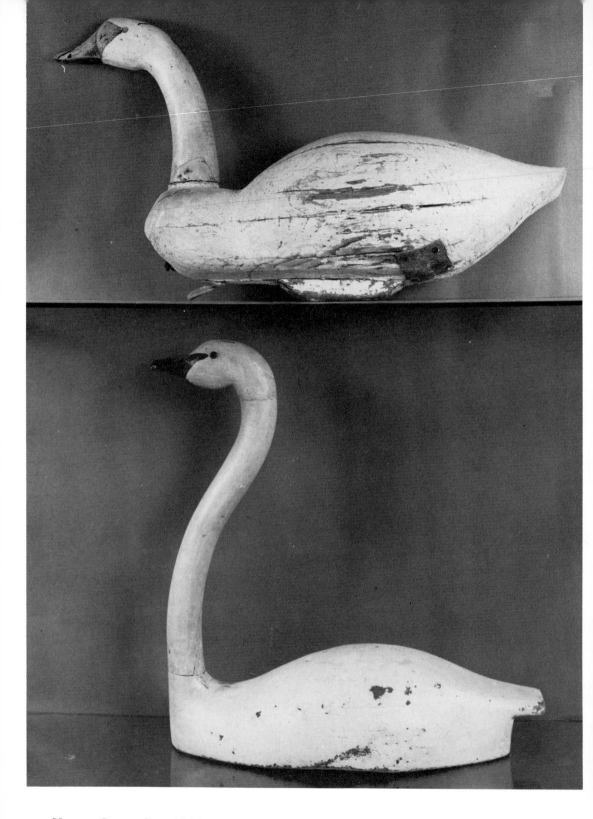

Upper: Swan circa 1900 — maker unknown, Dorchester County, Maryland — old repaint.

Lower: Swan circa 1890 — Orem Family, Dorchester County, Maryland — old repaint.

Upper: Swan circa 1935 — John Vickers, Cambridge, Maryland — original paint.
Lower: Swan circa 1950's — Elliot Bros., Easton, Maryland — original paint — cork model.

Upper: Swan circa 1900 — maker unknown, Dorchester County, Maryland — old paint. Apparently made by the same man who made the goose in Plate 3.

Lower: Swan circa 1910 — maker unknown, Dorchester County, Maryland — old repaint.

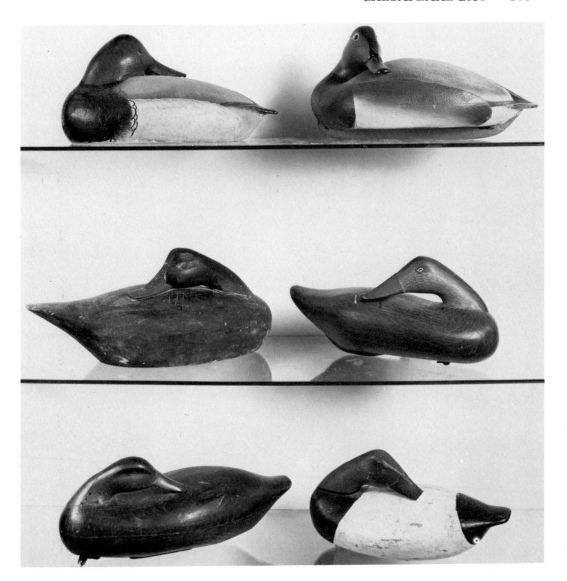

Upper left: Canvasback drake circa 1948 — L. T. Ward and Bros., Crisfield, Maryland — original paint — rare sleeper model.

Upper right: Canvasback hen circa 1948 — L. T. Ward and Bros., Crisfield, Maryland — original paint — an exceptionally fine and rare sleeper decoy.

Middle left: Black duck circa 1940's — maker unknown, Rock Hall, Maryland — old repaint.

Middle right: Black duck circa 1940 — Robert F. McGaw, Havre de Grace, Maryland — old repaint.

Lower right: Canvasback drake circa 1946 — Clarence Webb, Elkton, Maryland — old repaint.

Lower left: Black duck circa 1920 — maker unknown, South Jersey — repaint by Lem Ward — hollow white cedar.

Drake scaup circa 1946 — L. T. Ward and Brother, Crisfield, Maryland — original paint — excellent, early low back balsa model. The first Ward decoy purchased by the author.

Below, J.J. Audubon, engraving of Scaup Duck, courtesy The Old Print Shop, New York City.

Mallard hen circa 1932 — L. T. Ward & Bros., Crisfield, Maryland — original paint.

Redhead drake circa 1918 — L. T. Ward, Crisfield, Maryland — repaint by Lem.
The Ward "fat Jaw" model.

Redhead drake, circa 1918 — L.T. Ward, Crisfield, Maryland — repaint by Lem. The Ward "fat jaw" model, two views.

Upper: Drake and hen pintail circa 1925 — L. T. Ward & Bro., Crisfield, Maryland — repaint by Lem — rare hump-back model.

Middle: Hen and drake pintail circa 1936 — L. T. Ward & Bro., Crisfield, Maryland — original paint — classic 1936 model.

Lower: Two drake pintails circa 1936 — L. T. Ward & Bro., Crisfield, Maryland — original paint.

Upper: Hen and drake American goldeneye circa 1948 — L. T. Ward & Bro., Crisfield, Maryland — original paint.

Middle: Hen and drake scaup circa 1948 — L. T. Ward & Bro., Crisfield, Maryland — original paint.

Lower: Hen and drake canvasback circa 1948 — L. T. Ward & Bro., Crisfield, Maryland — original paint.

Upper: Drake and hen canvasback circa 1928 — L. T. Ward & Bro., Crisfield, Maryland — original paint — Knob head model.

Middle: Drake and hen canvasback, circa 1934 — L. T. Ward & Bro., Crisfield, Maryland — original paint — open water model.

Lower: Drake and hen canvasback circa 1925 — L. T. Ward & Bro., Crisfield, Maryland — original paint — raised wing model.

Upper: Drake and hen redhead circa 1932 — L. T. Ward & Bro., Crisfield, Maryland — original paint.

Middle left: Drake scaup circa 1935 — L. T. Ward & Bro., Crisfield, Maryland — original paint — high head model.

Middle right: Drake canvasback circa 1935 — L. T. Ward & Bro., Crisfield, Maryland — original paint. Formerly in the rig of Glenn L. Martin.

Lower left: Hen mallard circa 1941 — L. T. Ward and Bro., Crisfield, Maryland — original paint.

Lower right: Drake canvasback circa 1932 — L. T. Ward and Bro., Crisfield, Maryland — original paint — slot back model.

Upper: Hen and drake scaup circa 1936 — L. T. Ward & Bro., Crisfield, Maryland — original paint.

Middle: Drake and hen goldeneye, circa 1936 — L. T. Ward & Bro., Crisfield, Maryland — repaint by Lem Ward.

Lower left: Scaup drake circa 1936 — L. T. Ward & Bro., Crisfield, Maryland — original paint — Fox Island Gun Club model.

Lower right: Drake goldeneye circa 1936 — L. T. Ward & Bro., Crisfield, Maryland — original paint — "gathered breast" model.

Upper: Two drake goldeneyes circa 1922 — Lloyd Sterling, Crisfield, Maryland — original paint. These birds are referred to locally as "king bee divers".

Middle left: Hen goldeneye circa 1920 — Lloyd Sterling, Crisfield, Maryland — original paint.

Middle right: Drake goldeneye circa 1920 — the Sterling Family, Crisfield, Maryland — original paint.

Lower: Hen and drake goldeneye circa 1920 — Will Sterling, Crisfield, Maryland — original paint — another pair of "king bee divers".

Drake scaup circa 1918 — L. T. Ward, Crisfield, Maryland — repaint — head on view of Lem's "fat Jaw" model.

Drake scaup circa 1918 — L. T. Ward, Crisfield, Maryland — repaint — Lem's "fat Jaw" model.

Drake redhead circa 1930 — Ward Brothers, Lem and Steve, Crisfield, Maryland — original paint — Fox Island Gun Club model.

Black duck circa 1921 — Lem Ward, Crisfield, Maryland — original paint — high tail model with early scratch paint job.

Drake and hen canvasback circa 1948 — L. T. Ward and Brother, Crisfield, Maryland — a fine, oversize pair of balsa model Ward canvasbacks. Probably made for use on big water.

Canvasback hen and drake circa 1936 — L. T. Ward and Brother, Crisfield, Maryland — original paint. Lem and Steve's classic canvasbacks, among the most popular of all Ward Brothers decoys.

Upper: Hen and drake baldpates or American widgeon, circa 1948 — L. T. Ward & Bro., Crisfield, Maryland — original paint. The Ward's post-war model.

Middle: Drake and hen mallards circa 1948 — L. T. Ward & Bro., Crisfield, Maryland — original paint — balsa model.

Lower: Drake and hen pintails circa 1948 — L. T. Ward & Bro. Crisfield, Maryland — original paint — balsa model.

Upper left: Black duck circa 1932 — L. T. Ward & Bro., Crisfield, Maryland — original paint.

Upper right: Black duck circa 1936 — L. T. Ward & Bro., Crisfield, Maryland — original paint.

Middle left: Black duck circa 1935 — L. T. Ward & Bro., Crisfield, Maryland — original paint.

Middle right: Black duck circa 1932 — L. T. Ward & Bro., Crisfield, Maryland — original paint — from the rig of the Bishops Head Gun Club, Dorchester County, Maryland.

Lower left: Black duck circa 1922 — L. T. Ward & Bro., Crisfield, Maryland — old repaint by Lem Ward.

Lower right: Black duck circa 1950 — L. T. Ward & Bro., Crisfield, Maryland — original paint.

Canvasback hen circa 1948 — L. T. Ward & Bro., Crisfield, Maryland — original paint. An exquisite piece, one of Lem's finest working decoys.

Black duck circa 1957 — L. T. Ward & Bro., Crisfield, Maryland — original paint.

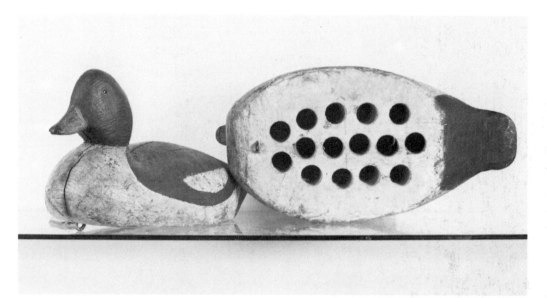

Hen and drake American goldeneye—same birds pictured on page 174, bottom showing method of lightening the decoys.

J.J. Audubon, engraving of Golden Eye Duck, courtesy The Old Print Shop, New York City.

Upper: Old squaw drake circa 1970 — L. T. Ward & Bro., Crisfield, Maryland — original paint.

Middle: Three surf scoters circa 1970 — L. T. Ward & Bro., Crisfield, Maryland — original paint.

Lower: Herring gull circa 1966 — L. T. Ward & Bro., Crisfield, Maryland — original paint.

Upper: Drake pintail circa 1935 — Lloyd Tyler, Crisfield, Maryland — original paint — a fine stylish pintail.

Middle: Drake pintail circa 1940's — maker unknown, Dorchester County, Maryland — original paint.

Lower: Drake pintail circa 1935 — Ira Hudson, Chincoteague, Virginia — original paint.

Upper: Canada goose circa 1932 — L. T. Ward & Bro., Crisfield, Maryland — old original paint — "big head" model.

Middle: Canada goose circa 1948 — L. T. Ward & Bro., Crisfield, Maryland — original paint — oversize balsa model.

Lower: Canada goose circa 1936 — L. T. Ward & Bro., Crisfield, Maryland — old repaint — raised wing carving — classic model.

Upper: Canada goose decoy circa 1930 — L. T. Ward & Bro., Crisfield, Maryland — original paint — low breast model. Note extremely long tail.

Middle: Canada goose circa 1925 — L. T. Ward, Crisfield, Maryland — repainted by Lem, 1965 — rare "snuggler" model.

Lower: Canada goose circa 1925 — L. T. Ward & Bro., Crisfield, Maryland — repainted by Lem — swimmer model.

Upper: Canada goose circa 1910 — maker unknown, Eastern Shore of Virginia — repainted by Ira Hudson — formerly in the rig of the Bob-O-Del Club.

Middle: Hutchins goose circa 1932 — L. T. Ward & Bro., Crisfield, Maryland — repainted — extremely rare species.

Lower: Canada goose circa 1925 — Ira Hudson, Chincoteague, Virginia — repainted by Hudson. Note raised wing carving. Formerly in the rig of the Bob-O-Del Club.

Upper: Canada goose circa 1890 — maker unknown, vicinity of Taylor's Island, Dorchester County, Maryland — old repaint. An exceptional early goose with wing carving on back and carved eyes.

Lower: Canada goose circa 1935 — Elliot Bros., Easton, Maryland — original paint — a caller model.

CHAPTER 6
Eastern shore of Virginia, Back Bay-Currituck Sound

Visiting the Eastern Shore of Virginia is like stepping into the past. From the Maryland line on down to Cape Charles, the impression of easy living in the "Old South" is ever present. Even along the commercialized sections of U. S. Highway 13, which splits the sixty mile long peninsula in half, one encounters an aura that is difficult to explain. Once you turn off the highway and amble on down to Locustville, Chincoteague, Modest Town, Guilford, or any of the dozens of other little seaside or bayside communities, the idea that you have left the modern world behind really strikes home. The beautiful early homes dating from the seventeenth century with their lovely gardens seem to invite you to stop in and visit awhile. The tiny general stores in each village where you can purchase a real, home cooked hamburger, or penny candy or a new fishing hat cast a mystifying spell over all who stop in. The endless marshes, golden in the fall even on an overcast day, with a pair of silken-winged blackies dropping into one of the innumerable creeks that wind their twisting tidal flow far into the depth of the cattails, beckon one to stay and taste the sport that they offer.

In the summer the flounder, the crabs, the country corn and the fresh tomatoes — never mind the mosquitos that sometimes appear bigger than the mockingbirds — lull the visitor into believing that he too need never return to that from which he has escaped.

Into this country of vast marshes and endless creeks, bounded on one shore by the mighty Chesapeake and on the other by the powerful Atlantic Ocean, God has seen fit to direct the black duck. And the men who populate this area have seen fit to direct their efforts toward hunting the black duck. Not only has God provided them with that duck, but also with the wiles needed to hunt him.

The predominate decoy found on the Eastern Shore is the black duck stool. This species represented the primary output of most of the makers, and although decoys for most ducks and brant and geese are found, black duck decoys are the most numerous. A valuable collection that would require a respectable amount of time and outlay of money, could be built by collecting just black duck decoys made on the Eastern Shore of Virginia. The decoys by most of the major makers here, men like Ira Hudson, Charles Birch, Dave Watson, Doug Jester, Miles Hancock and the Cobb Family are in great demand all over the country and are commanding premium prices.

The majority of the decoys made on the shore were solid. Only a few makers, apparently influenced by the numerous New Jersey coast decoys used down there, produced hollow carved two-piece birds. They were made of white cedar, pine, cypress, and cottonwood — the preference for woods in that order — with an occasional rig of balsa wood. Ira Hudson made both solid and hollow birds, and examples of his decoys have been found in each of the woods listed above. Charlie Birch made most all of his decoys hollow and his style resembled the New Jersey coast decoy. A few of his birds are known that are solid. Miles Hancock and Doug Jester decoys were all made solid.

The paint on many Eastern Shore of Virginia decoys was rather elaborate, and scratch painting was employed extensively. In some cases the paint jobs bordered on the gaudy, in others they are very simple and drab. Original paint on decoys from this region is very desirable and important and greatly increases the value of the decoy. Today, Ira Hudson decoys in original paint command huge prices when they can be found.

A little farther down the peninsula lie a string of barrier islands offshore between the mainland and the Atlantic Ocean. One of these islands was settled by the Nathan Cobb Family soon after their move to the Eastern Shore from Cape Cod in 1833. Nathan and his three sons Nathan Jr., Warren, and Albert apparently all made the Cobb Island type decoy, and distinguishing who made which at this stage would be academic at best. Elkaneh Cobb, son of Nathan Jr., also made decoys in the family style, and those with an "E" cut into the bottom are attributed to him. A number of other Cobb Family decoys with an old style "N" cut into the bottom are considered to have been made by Nathan Cobb, but whether they were by Nathan Sr. or Nathan Jr. is unknown. Most of the wooden stool made on the island were for black duck, brant, Canada goose, and blackhead. A few other species by the Cobbs are known, but they are unusually rare. Other settlers on the island in later years made decoys patterned after the design of the Cobb birds. Today all of these similarly styled decoys with the bulky oversized bodies and split wing and tail carving are referred to as Cobb Island decoys and are very desirable.

The Eastern Shore continues on down to Kiptopeke on its southern tip and decoys were made all along this section of the seaside and on up the bayside by the watermen and duck hunters that lived in the small towns of this region. On the southern end toward Cape Charles, the families of the Wendells, Bulls, Wilkins, Andrews, and Parks all made duck decoys for their own use. On the bayside around Harborton, a small fishing village on the shores of the Chesapeake, several carvers were active. They were John Dize, Ike Phillips, and Garland Turner. Many more decoys were made in this lower region that have as yet been unidentified as to the maker, but are still very collectible as unknowns.

The Eastern Shore of Virginia is eight hundred square miles of some of the most beautiful tidewater country that anyone could ever hope to enjoy. It is an early historical section of our country, settled by the British in 1614, and it retains much of its colonial enchantment to this day. It is a narrow strip of fast land edged with expansive marshes opening to numerous bays, creeks, inlets, and guts, prime waterfowl country that has played host for centuries to the wildfowl that were lured past the inviting waters of Maryland's Eastern Shore just to the north.

Just across the Chesapeake Bay via the bridge-tunnel system lies the metropolitan Norfolk — Virginia Beach area and a short distance farther south one encounters the Back Bay, Virginia — Currituck Sound, North Carolina territory. Long known for its famous waterfowl gunning, this region carries a history dating from the mid-Victorian era, when duck shooting was enjoying its finest hour in America. The wealthy tycoons, who had amassed great fortunes developing our country during its tremendous growth in industry, were accustomed to the best of everything and they could well afford it. They flocked to the Back Bay — Currituck Sound area to reap the benefits of the unbelievably good canvasback and redhead shooting. A watery expanse, similar in character to its justly famous neighbor, the Susquehanna Flats, abounding in the succulent wild celery so irresistible to the ducks, and surrounded by extensive marshes that provided nurseries for the finfish and shellfish which abundantly populated these waters, much of the Back Bay - Currituck section was soon in the hands of the millionaire sportsmen.

Many hunting clubs were established on the islands and points as the land was purchased. The railroads, steamboat lines, and later, the automobile carried the owners and their friends south from New York, Philadelphia, Baltimore, and Norfolk to engage in the popular sport of duck hunting and fishing. The Goulds, Knapps, Eastmans, Disstons, and our famous sportsman — president Grover Cleveland experienced the memorable gunning there.

The care and management of the clubs, their grounds, blinds, and equipment, fell to the local residents of the area. Most of them had hunted and worked on the water all of their lives and it was only natural that they would be retained to do the guiding, to provide the decoys, and to generally keep an eye on things for the absentee landlords. Many of the men made their own decoys and today a few of the names are outstanding in the decoy collecting world, John Williams, the Waterfield Family, and Ivey Stevens in Virginia, and the famous brothers Lee and Lem Dudley, Ned Burgess, Mitchell Fulcher, and Alvirah Wright in North Carolina.

Actually, the two bodies of water are connected — the Virginia-North Carolina state line splits Knotts Island in half — and the fact that many of the makers in this region lived their lives at different times in each state, makes it difficult to call them North Carolina or Virginia carvers.

The decoys tended to be oversized, bulky stool, made solid, so they would ride well and could be seen for some distance on the big bodies of water. Often referred to as crude and rough, I much prefer and rather like the description given to these decoys by Mr. Jim Lewis of Goldsboro, North Carolina, a serious historian of the decoys of his state and a fine southern gentleman, when he says "Instead of crude and rough, they might more fairly have been described as rugged and functional."

Many of them had very interesting and appealing lines. The primitive design in the majority of birds lends a very attractive appearance. Some, as in the case of the Dudleys and John Williams, rank among the most exceptional and important decoys today.

The painting of the decoys consisted of a very simple but effective pattern. The paint on the birds in this region is probably as elementary as in any other decoy making area along the coast. And for good reason. Large rigs were employed in conjunction with the batteries and stake blinds on the big open water and the birds were subjected to rough handling as often occurs when great numbers of decoys are rigged out or are being picked up. This hard usage necessitated the frequent painting of the decoys to maintain their fresh and bright appearance. The easier the pattern that needed to be re-applied, the quicker the job was finished. There are no definite paint characteristics common to the decoys in the Back Bay — Currituck Sound area that would help in their identification as to locale.

A very typical identifying aid is found in the ballast weight that is attached to a great number of the decoys from down here though, and it can only be described as a rectangular piece of iron with a hump in the middle of the half that protrudes down from the bottom of the decoy. It is usually three to five inches long and one to one and one half inches wide.

It is made of iron cast in the local foundries of the region. Also cast here were anchor weights and iron wing decoys similar in design to those made and used on the Susquehanna Flats.

The major species in this area for which decoys were made are canvasback, redhead, Canada goose, brant, widgeon, and ruddy duck. Very few mallard or black duck decoys are found. Farther south in the Pamlico Sound territory pintail decoys are quite numerous.

On an ending note, it is appropriate to say that all of the decoys of Back Bay and Currituck Sound, carried to prominence nationally by a handful of old time carvers, are beginning to receive the attention they have long deserved by a growing number of decoy collectors around the country.

Drake canvasback circa 1925 — Ira Hudson, Chincoteague, Virginia — original paint. An early, very fine canvasback decoy by the unexcelled leader of the Chincoteague carvers. Note the swirled breast paint, the tack eyes, the bill carving, and the fluted tail, all distinctive Hudson characteristics.

Drake canvasback circa 1940 — Ira Hudson, Chincoteague, Virginia — mint original condition. This decoy has never been used, is a reasonably rare species by Hudson, and is extremely desirable to collectors everywhere.

Drake canvasback circa 1930 — Ira Hudson, Chincoteague, Virginia — mint original condition — another, different model Hudson can.

Upper: Hen and drake American goldeneye circa 1935 — Ira Hudson, Chincoteague, Virginia — original paint.

Middle left: Black duck circa 1920 — Ira Hudson, Chincoteague, Virginia — original paint — an unusual undersize Hudson black duck.

Middle right: Bufflehead drake circa 1925 — Ira Hudson, Chincoteague, Virginia — old repaint.

Lower: Hen and drake scaup circa 1915 — Ira Hudson, Chincoteague, Virginia — original paint. A near mint pair of "banjo tail" blackheads.

Upper: Hen and drake scaup circa 1950's — Delbert "Cigar" Daisey, Chincoteague, Virginia — original paint.

Middle: Two drake scaup circa 1920's — Ira Hudson, Chincoteague, Virginia — original paint — round bottom, "banjo" tail style.

Lower: Hen and drake scaup circa 1940 — Ira Hudson, Chincoteague, Virginia — original paint — later flat bottom model.

Upper: Black duck circa 1910 — Ira Hudson, Chincoteague, Virginia — original paint — solid.

Middle: Black duck circa 1915 — Charles Birch, Willis Wharf, Virginia — original paint — hollow.

Lower: Black duck circa 1900 — Dave "Umbrella" Watson, Chincoteague, Virginia — original paint — hollow.

Upper: Black duck circa 1915 — Ira Hudson, Chincoteague, Virginia — original paint. Very nice hollow model by Hudson — fluted tail.

Middle: Redhead drake circa 1940 — Douglas Jester, Chincoteague, Virginia — mint original paint and condition.

Lower: Goldeneye drake circa 1920 — Ira Hudson, Chincoteague, Virginia — original paint — rare species by Hudson.

Upper left: Hen hooded merganser circa 1940's — Doug Jester, Chincoteague, Virginia — original paint.

Upper right: Hen redhead circa 1940's — Doug Jester, Chincoteague, Virginia — original paint.

Middle left: Black duck: circa 1940's — Doug Jester, Chincoteague, Virginia — original paint.

Middle right: Drake mallard circa 1940's — Doug Jester, Chincoteague, Virginia — original paint.

Lower: Canada goose circa 1940's — Doug Jester, Chincoteague, Virginia — original paint.

Upper: Drake canvasback circa 1930's — Ira Hudson, Chincoteague, Virginia — original paint.

Middle: Drake and hen canvasback circa 1940's — Douglas Jester, Chincoteague, Virginia — original mint condition.

Lower left: Black duck circa 1940's — Douglas Jester, Chincoteague, Virginia — original paint.

Lower right: Redhead drake circa 1940's — Douglas Jester, Chincoteague, Virginia — original paint.

Upper: Drake goldeneye circa 1920 — Douglas Jester, Chincoteague, Virginia — original paint.

Middle: Drake pintail circa 1930 — Douglas Jester, Chincoteague, Virginia — original paint — mint condition.

Lower: Hen pintail circa 1930 — Douglas Jester, Chincoteague, Virginia — original paint — mint condition.

Upper: Brant, circa 1940's — Miles Hancock, Chincoteague, Virginia — in mint original paint and condition — in the rig of the Bob-O-Del Club.

Middle left: Scaup drake, circa 1940's — Miles Hancock, Chincoteague, Virginia — original paint.

Middle right: Black duck, circa 1930's — Miles Hancock, Chincoteague, Virginia — original paint.

Lower left: Hen red breasted merganser, circa 1940's — Miles Hancock, Chincoteague, Virginia — original paint.

Lower right: Drake baldpate, circa 1940's — Miles Hancock, Chincoteague, Virginia — original paint.

Note: All decoys on this page were formerly in the rig of the Bob-O-Del Club.

Upper: Hen and drake pintail, circa 1940's — Miles Hancock, Chincoteague, Virginia — original paint.

Middle: Hen and drake goldeneye, circa 1940's — Miles Hancock, Chincoteague, Virginia — original paint.

Lower: Drake and hen bufflehead, circa 1940's — Miles Hancock, Chincoteague, Virginia — original paint.

Upper: Hen and drake red breasted merganser, circa 1940's — Miles Hancock, Chincoteague, Virginia — original paint.

Middle left: Drake baldpate, circa 1940's — Miles Hancock, Chincoteague, Virginia — original paint.

Middle right: Coot, circa 1940's — Miles Hancock, Chincoteague, Virginia — original paint.

Lower: Two black ducks, circa 1940's — Miles Hancock, Chincoteague, Virginia — original paint. Note rare sleeper model on right.

Upper: Hen and drake canvasback, circa 1940's — Miles Hancock, Chincoteague, Virginia — original paint.

Middle: Drake and hen scaup, cira 1940's — Miles Hancock, Chincoteague, Virginia — original paint.

Lower: Hen and drake redhead, circa 1940's — Miles Hancock, Chincoteague, Virginia — original paint.

Brant, circa 1920 — Ira Hudson, Chincoteague, Virginia — old repaint.

Upper: Brant, circa 1925 — Ira Hudson, Chincoteague, Virginia — old repaint by Ira Hudson.

Middle: Brant, circa 1925 — Ira Hudson, Chincoteague, Virginia — old New Jersey repaint.

Lower: Brant, circa 1925 — Ira Hudson, Chincoteague, Virginia — original paint.

Upper: Two brant, circa 1920 — Ira Hudson, Chincoteague, Virginia — old repaint — "crooked neck" model. These heads and necks were usually made of a driftwood root.

Middle left: Brant, circa 1920 — Charles Birch, Willis Wharf, Virginia — original paint — hollow carved.

Middle right: Brant, circa 1910 — Dave "Umbrella" Watson, Chincoteague, Virginia — original paint — hollow.

Lower left: Brant, circa 1940's — Miles Hancock, Chincoteague, Virginia — original paint.

Lower right: Brant, circa 1946 — Doug Jester, Chincoteague, Virginia — old repaint.

Upper: Canada goose, circa 1930's — Ira Hudson, Chincoteague, Virginia — old repaint. Note hollow three piece construction and raised wing carving.

Lower: Canada goose, circa 1930's — Ira Hudson, Chincoteague, Virginia — old repaint. Note hollow three piece construction and lack of raised wing carving.

Upper: Canada goose circa 1930 — Ira Hudson, Chincoteague, Virginia — some original paint — an extremely nice hollow goose decoy, one of the finest heads known on a Hudson goose.

Middle: Canada goose circa 1925 — Ira Hudson, Chincoteague, Virginia — original paint.

Lower: Canada goose circa 1920 — Ira Hudson, Chincoteague, Virginia — old repaint — note the nice hissing head and raised wing carving.

Upper: Canada goose circa 1930's — Ira Hudson, Chincoteague, Virginia — old repaint, rare hissing head model.

Middle: Canvasback drake circa 1930's — Ira Hudson, Chincoteague, Virginia — original paint.

Lower: Brant circa 1920's — Ira Hudson, Chincoteague, Virginia — old repaint — balsa "Sleeper" model.

Upper: Canada goose, circa 1938 — Ira Hudson, Chincoteague, Virginia — original paint.

Middle: Canada goose, circa 1925 — Charles Birch, Willis Wharf, Virginia — old repaint — beautiful style that captures the grace of the Birch swan.

Lower: Canada goose, circa 1900 — Dave "Umbrella" Watson, Chincoteague, Virginia — old repaint.

Upper: Two drake scaup circa 1915 — Charles Birch, Willis Wharf, Virginia — old repaints.

Middle left: Pintail drake circa 1920 — Charles Birch, Willis Wharf, Virginia — cleaned to original paint — a rare and valuable addition to Birch history. This is the first pintail by Birch recorded in a collection.

Middle right: Drake scaup circa 1925 — Charles Birch, Willis Wharf, Virginia — original paint.

Lower left: Drake American goldeneye circa 1925 — Charles Birch, Willis Wharf, Virginia — original paint.

Lower right: Black duck circa 1920 — Charles Birch, Willis Wharf, Virginia — original paint.

Upper: Drake and hen scaup circa 1915 — Charles Birch, Willis Wharf, Virginia — original paint — hollow.

Middle: Canvasback drake circa 1920 — Miles Hancock, Chincoteague, Virginia — original paint.

Lower: Canvasback drake circa 1900 — Dave "Umbrella" Watson, Chincoteague, Virginia — old repaint — rare species — hollow model.

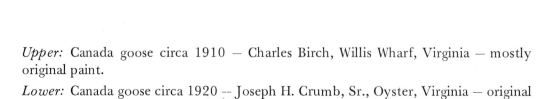

Upper: Canada goose circa 1910 — Charles Birch, Willis Wharf, Virginia — mostly original paint.

Lower: Canada goose circa 1920 — Joseph H. Crumb, Sr., Oyster, Virginia — original paint — hollow decoy.

Upper: Canada goose circa 1930 — Douglas Jester, Chincoteague, Virginia — original paint — hole drilled in bottom for use as stick-up as well as a floater.

Lower: Canada goose circa 1900 — Walter Brady, Oyster, Virginia — old repaint.

Upper: Swan circa 1920 — Charles Birch, Willis Wharf, Virginia — original paint. A rare and very desirable decoy — one of a rig made for use in Talbot County, Maryland, this bird is probably the finest member of that rig.

Lower: Swan circa 1900 — maker unknown, Dorchester County, Maryland — old repaint.

Upper: Black duck circa 1940 — Douglas Jester, Chincoteague, Virginia — original paint.

Middle: Black duck circa 1910 — Ira Hudson, Chincoteague, Virginia — original paint.

Lower: Black duck circa 1900 — Elkenah Cobb, Cobb Island, Virginia — old repaint — carved "E" in bottom for Elkenah.

Brant circa 1890 — Nathan Cobb, Jr., Cobb Island, Virginia — original paint. An exceptionally fine and rare decoy, note the split tail and wing carving and the extended reaching head and neck.

Pintail hen circa 1930 — probably by Ira Hudson's son, Norman — Chincoteague, Virginia — original paint — an excellent Virginia-Eastern shore decoy in very fine original condition. Note the head position, sharply turned to the right, and the imaginative paint pattern.

Upper: Brant, circa 1890 — the Cobb Family, Cobb Island, Virginia — original paint.

Middle: Brant, circa 1890 — the Cobb Family, Cobb Island, Virginia — old repaint.

Lower: Brant, circa 1900 — maker unknown, the Eastern Shore of Virginia — old repaint.

Upper: Black duck circa 1925 — Ira Hudson, Chincoteague, Virginia — old repaint — solid.

Middle: Black duck circa 1890 — maker unknown, Hog Island, Virginia — old repaint — solid.

Lower: Black duck circa 1885 — Nathan Cobb, Cobb's Island, Virginia — original paint — hollow — marked with an "N" in bottom for Nathan.

Upper: Scaup drake circa 1900 — Doughty Family, Hog Island, Virginia — old working repaint — inletted neck.

Middle: Scaup drake circa 1910 — Lee and Lem Dudley, Knotts Island, Virginia — old working repaint.

Lower: Black duck circa 1910 — Charles Birch, Willis Wharf, Virginia — original paint — hollow model.

Drake scaup circa 1890 — maker unknown, Eastern Shore, Virginia — old repaint — a very round, fat little duck decoy that has a lot of appeal.

Goldeneye hen, circa 1900 — maker unknown, Lower Eastern Shore of Maryland or Eastern Shore of Virginia — old repaint. An outstanding example of decoy folk art.

Drake canvasback circa 1890 — Lem Dudley, Knotts Island, North Carolina — old repaint — a classic southern bird. The ultimate in North Carolina decoys.

Canada goose circa 1890 — Lem Dudley, Knotts Island, North Carolina — old repaint. A remarkable goose decoy which exhibits the skilled craft of the most famous North Carolina decoy maker. Collection of Refuge Waterfowl Museum, Chincoteague, Virginia.

Ruddy duck circa 1890 — John Williams, Cedar Island, Virginia — original paint. An exceptionally fine little decoy, made to lure the "dollar ducks" for market on Back Bay, Virginia. Collection of Refuge Waterfowl Museum, Chincoteague, Virginia.

Upper: Canvasback drake circa 1915 — Alvirah Wright, Duck, North Carolina — original paint.

Middle: Redhead drake circa 1920 — Robert Brothers, Church's Island, North Carolina — original paint.

Lower: Redhead drake circa 1915 — Alvirah Wright, Duck, North Carolina — old repaint.

Upper: Canvasback drake circa 1915 — Ned Burgess, Church's Island, North Carolina — original paint.

Middle: Canvasback drake circa 1920 — Ivy Stevens, Cedar Island, Back Bay, Virginia — old repaint.

Lower: Canvasback drake circa 1925 — Wilton Walker, Tulls Bay, North Carolina — old repaint.

Note: The above three birds are typical of the oversize, solid decoys used on Back Bay through North Carolina.

Upper: Canvasback hen circa 1930 — Bob Morse, Church's Island, North Carolina — original paint.

Lower: Redhead drake circa 1925 — maker unknown, Church's Island, North Carolina — old repaint.

Left: Redhead drake circa 1920 — Mitchell Fulcher, Stacy, North Carolina — original paint.

Right: Scaup drake circa 1920 — Mitchell Fulcher, Stacy, North Carolina — original paint.

Both decoys marked with initials of the maker — "M.F." in bottom.

Below, J.J. Audubon's engraving, courtesy The Old Print Shop, New York City.

CHAPTER 7
Makers

ALGARD, CARROLL CLEVELAND "WALLY", *1883-1959, CHARLESTOWN, MARYLAND* — Wally Algard was a sportsman all of his life fishing, hunting and guiding on the Northeast River and the Susquehanna Flats. He made decoys for his own use rather than for a living and as such his birds are more scarce than those of the other makers from this community. He made only canvasback decoys and they are very distinctive in appearance. They have a shelf carving and a straight tail in the middle of the body common to the Cecil County school of carvers. Most of his birds exhibit an abnormal hump on the back just before the tail that is more pronounced than in other decoys made here. Many also have an underslung bill carving that helps to identify Algard's birds.

BARNARD, CHARLES NELSON, *1876-1958, HAVRE DE GRACE, MARYLAND* — Charlie Barnard was born in Havre de Grace, the son of a sea captain in 1876. He left school at the age of nine to go to work on his father's ship and except for a period of time working for the Pennsylvania Railroad, he spent the rest of his life on the water. He is noted particularly for his high headed canvasback decoys that were used as tollers in a sinkbox rig. He made a few redhead and black duck decoys that were hollow, a very unusual characteristic for the Flats. There is one ruddy duck decoy made in 1910 in the family collection and a grandson can remember hunting over a handful of "mo-hen" or coot decoys made by his grandfather. He carved a shelf on his birds which is a departure from the normal Havre de Grace style. The tails on his decoys are also different in that they are at the top of the body but extend straight out rather than being upswept. Blackheads round out his number of species. Barnard made his last major rig in 1937 for Senator Millard Tydings of Havre de Grace.

BARNES, GEORGE WASHINGTON "WASH", *1861-1915, CARPENTER'S POINT, MARYLAND* — "Wash" Barnes with his four brothers owned and operated a fishing camp at Carpenter's Point, which is located on the Susquehanna Flats at the mouth of the Northeast River. The brothers enjoyed hunting and Perry K. Barnes maintained a sink box rig for their use. A number of old decoys branded with "P. K. BARNES" in the bottom have surfaced as the remnants of this rig. G.W. Barnes' decoy heads resemble closely those of Scott Jackson and they are difficult to tell from one another, yet the bodies of these two carvers are entirely different. Barnes' bodies display a well defined and rather sharp chine all the way around the circumference of the body, and the tail is not nearly as salient as those of Jackson's. George W. Barnes made, so far as is known, only canvasback and black ducks.

BARNES, SAMUEL TREADWAY, *1847-1926, HARVE DE GRACE, MARYLAND* — Mention the name Sam Barnes and most collectors think of his famous swan decoy, formerly in the Joel Barber collection, and now, in Shelburne Museum. Sam Barnes was a duck hunter, fisherman, and prolific decoy maker from Havre de Grace, Maryland. He made Canada geese, canvasback, redheads, blackheads, and black ducks. His earlier decoys were long bodied with straight sides and present a squarish appearance. His heads have definite flat areas on each side of the face and down the crown into the bill in the front. His later birds were more rounded in the bodies and the heads, but the "flats" remained as before. Sam Barnes also made cork decoys, with a pine head and bottom board, in Canada goose, canvasback, blackhead, redhead, and black duck. They are probably the earliest cork decoys made on the Chesapeake Bay. He painted wing and feather patterns on all of his decoys. Sam Barnes died in February, 1926, and was the first burial Madison Mitchell had out of a brand new hearse he bought that year.

BIRDSALL, CAPT. JESSE, *c. 1852-c. 1929, BARNEGAT, NEW JERSEY* — Typical Barnegat style decoys — hollow cedar, noticeable eye area indentation and a high back and tail. His bottoms were flatter than any others from the Barnegat area. His decoys and those of Hen Grants' are very similar in style and appearance, except for the flatter bottoms. Decoy species known by him are bufflehead, goldeneye, black duck, scaup, brant and Canada goose.

BLAIR, JOHN, *carved circa 1860-1880, PHILADELPHIA, PENNSYLVANIA* — The decoys attributed to John Blair of Philadelphia, Pennsylvania and Cecil County, Maryland are classics and rank with the most beautifully made decoys in this country. They are early, hollow carved, sleek decoys with exceptional paint on them. Mr. Blair spent a considerable amount of time at his farm just off the Susquehanna Flats in Cecil County, Maryland, and a number of the Blair decoys have turned up in this area. He was a contemporary of John "Daddy" Holly of Havre de Grace and they undoubtably met on the "ducking grounds." There are teal and mallard decoys in existence today known to have been made by John Holly and their original paint bears striking similarities to the paint on the Blair decoys. It is obvious to this collector that one or the other of these gentlemen was influenced by the other in his paint patterns. Perhaps a clue to the Blair mystery lies hidden here. Decoys attributed to Blair include mallards, black ducks, pintails, green and blue wing teal, widgeon, bluebills, and Canada geese.

BOYD, TAYLOR, *1856-1946, PERRYVILLE, MARYLAND* — Taylor Boyd was a carpenter born in Perryville in 1958. His decoys exemplify the difference between the Cecil County school and the Havre de Grace school of carvers. Each identifying characteristic of the Cecil County birds is evident in his decoys. Other distinctive aids to identification are a definite flat on the forehead running into the bill, mandible carving, and a notch on each side of the tail where it joins the body. This is an unfailing mark on his decoys. He made canvasback, redheads, and black ducks.

BURGESS, NED, *1863-1956, CHURCH'S ISLAND, VIRGINIA* — Ned Burgess was a prolific decoy maker from the town of Water Lily on Church's Island. He made a decoy that has attracted today's collector in all parts of the country and has provided a fine North Carolina specimen for those who can't find or afford a Dudley or Williams. His decoys have not received the credit they are worthy of, but their time is coming.

Burgess must have been a boat builder as the style of his birds shows the influence of boat design. The bodies are long and slender and resemble the hull of a skiff. His tails were high, on top of the body, and are undercut by several inches. His heads are upright and reared back with an alert attitude. Enough examples remain in original paint to make the hunt interesting. Decoy species known by Burgess are canvasback, redhead, blackhead, pintail, mallard, ruddy, and coots.

Ned Burgess, Church's Island, North Carolina — Hen Pintail showing the standard iron ballast commonly used on decoys from the Back Bay-Currituck Sound area.

THE COBB FAMILY

Nathan Cobb Sr. moved from Cape Cod, Massachusetts in 1833 to the Eastern Shore of Virginia with his ailing wife and three young sons, Nathan, Jr., Warren, and Albert. Shortly after moving to Virginia, the family acquired an offshore island, which was promptly named Cobb's Island, and here they all finally settled and began developing their gunning camp for visiting duck and goose shooters. The island was a refuge for the teeming wildfowl that engulfed the Eastern Shore of Virginia each spring and fall and because of the multitudes that flocked there, gunning was easy, and there was little need for decoys. Shooting finally began to take its toll and as the birds' numbers decreased and they grew more wary, wooden decoys became necessary to lure enough ducks and geese into range to provide ample sport for the guests. Thus, the Cobb Island style of decoy was originated by these transplanted New Englanders and despite its different design has survived through the last one hundred years to be totally identified with and take its place among the decoys of the Eastern Shore of Virginia.

The style tends toward a slightly oversized, bulky decoy made in two halves, hollowed, and with a prominent, in most cases, raised wing carving. Most are very round and are said to have been made out of the spars of the sailing ships salvaged by the Cobb Family around their island. The heads are found in any number of positions and are extremely interesting. Made of holly roots and other pieces of correctly shaped driftwood, they were made as reachers, feeders, straight heads, and tucked heads. The paint on the Cobb Family decoys, whether original or otherwise, is relatively unimportant to most collectors. To own a Cobb in any condition would be a valuable addition to one's collection.

Apparently Nathan Cobb, Jr. was responsible for most of the decoys found with an "N" carved in the bottom and Elkenah, his son, the birds with an "E". Whoever would say for sure that Nathan Sr. did or did not make any decoys would probably be guessing. There are also Cobb decoys with an "A" in the bottom and these can be attributed to either Albert, who was a brother to Nathan Jr. or Arthur, their nephew.

Cobb decoys are known in the species of Canada goose, brant, black duck, blackhead, redhead, bufflehead, and merganser.

COCKEY, JIM, *1893-1971, STEVENSVILLE, MARYLAND* — Jim Cockey was born and raised on Kent Island in Stevensville at the eastern terminus of the Chesapeake Bay Bridge. He was a Bay boat builder and the influence is evident in the design of his duck decoys. They had a small flat area on the bottom and a dead rise, common to all bay built boats, rising to the chine near the top of the decoy. A long slim tail flowed from the middle of the body in a style similar to the Cecil County decoys at the head of the Bay. There was also a shelf carving on which the head and neck rested. All of Jim's decoys were made solid out of white cedar or pine. He is known to have made canvasback, blackhead, redhead, and a few swan.

CRUMB, JOSEPH H., *1881-1935, OYSTER, VIRGINIA* — Joe Crumb guided hunting and fishing parties out of Oyster, Virginia, a small waterfront village on Cobb Island Bay. He often hunted and fished with his neighbors across the bay, the Cobb Family. He made hollow, two-piece decoys similar in design to the New Jersey coast decoys — many of which were hunted in his area. At the time of this writing only Canada geese, black duck, and goldeneye are known by Joseph Crumb.

CURRIER, JAMES A., *1886-1971, HAVRE DE GRACE, MARYLAND* — Jim Currier started working for the postal department as a young man and retired many years later as postmaster. He made decoys for his own use and as a sideline while working at the Post Office. He made a very fine working decoy and his early high necked canvasbacks would enhance any collector's shelf. His decoys had a very distinctive head and bill carving that becomes easy to recognize as one familiarizes himself with the decoys used on the Susquehanna Flats. His bills exhibit a "Roman nose" appearance that is quite pronounced in most birds. His wing and feather painting is feathery and more lightly done than others of a similar nature. In addition to cans, Jim Currier made Canada geese, redheads, blackheads, mallards, black ducks, pintail, and green winged teal.

DAWSON, JOHN, *1889-1959, TRENTON, NEW JERSEY* — John Dawson spent most of his time on Duck Island in the Delaware River near Trenton and he came to know the waterfowl that traveled the river well. He brought all of his skill as a carpenter and woodworker into play in the making of his finely constructed, two-piece hollow decoys. His birds were beautifully finished with a paint job that borders on the unbelievable. His patterned designs and blend of colors produced a bird that was very showy, but extremely natural looking. He is known to have made canvasback, redhead, pintail, mallard, widgeon, black duck, and red breasted merganser.

DUDLEY, LEE, *1861-1942* — **DUDLEY, LEM,** *1861-1932, KNOTTS ISLAND, NORTH CAROLINA* — Born on Knotts Island, North Carolina at the beginning of the War between the States, Lee and Lem Dudley grew up in a natural paradise teeming with wildfowl, game, and seafood of all descriptions. They gunned for the market and made a meagre living working on the water. They made decoys for their own hunting rig and at least that of one other man, a member of the neighboring Ballance family according to Bill Mackey in his book *American Bird Decoys.* The decoys were made before 1900 and apparently suffered hard usage, because few birds, if any, have been found with paint even close to original. They resemble closely the style and design of the early Susquehanna Flats decoy, except that most of them have a semblance of a wing outline carved back near the tail. The heads are very nicely done, but most collectors will agree they are hardly worth all of the praise lavished on them by Mr. Mackey in his aforementioned book. They are very rare and few have come on the market in recent years. When they do, they command premium prices as they are much sought after by decoy collectors everywhere. Decoys known by the Dudleys include Canada goose, canvasback, blackhead, redhead, widgeon, mallard, and green wing teal.

DYE, CAPTAIN BEN, *1821-1896, PERRYVILLE, MARYLAND* — Ben Dye was born in Monmouth, New Jersey on the site of what is now the Monmouth Race Track in 1821. He moved with his family to Cecil County, Maryland to settle at Stumps Point near Perryville on the shores of the Susquehanna Flats when he was a young boy. He earned his livelihood by hunting and fishing for the market and guiding sportsmen who came to the Flats as early as 1850 in search of the far famed duck hunting to be found there. He also made decoys for his own use and for sale to other guides and hunters in the area. Some of the nicest decoys to ever float on the Flats came from the hands of Ben Dye. They were all hand chopped and tended to be on the small side. The design and conformation of his decoys is outstanding. His earlier decoys were extremely flat and feature a little paddle tail while his later birds had very rounded, smooth symmetrical bodies with the tail less prominent. All of his heads and bills exhibited the finest carving and detail known in this region. He carved nostrils, mandibles, nail and ridge carving on his bills and smoothly done work where the bill joins the face. He is known to have made canvasback, redhead, blackhead, and black duck decoys.

Bottom of Ben Dye c.-1850 canvasback showing original Ben Dye cast lead ballast (upper lead) and brand of "P.K. BARNES".

DYE, JOSEPH E., *1870-1931, HAVRE DE GRACE, MARYLAND —* Joe Dye was born at Stump Point, Perryville, Maryland, the second son of Captain Ben Dye of Stump Point. Joe is listed as a Havre de Grace maker as he moved there in 1890 and made most of his decoys there. He made his living working on the Flats, fishing and hunting, and guiding the sportsmen who visited there. He often guided such famous and wealthy sportsmen as John Wanamaker, Jay Gould, and Henry Disston. He was the first gunner in Havre de Grace to own and hunt with a Browning automatic. He occasionally hunted out of a double sinkbox surrounded by approximately five hundred decoys which were practically all drakes as he painted few hens. Out of an entire rig of blackheads in original paint discovered by the author, not one was painted as a hen. Joe Dye also used the deadly ice box for black duck shooting when the Flats froze over.

His decoys are completely unlike the decoys of the Havre de Grace school of carvers. It is only natural that he would copy his father's design, that of the Cecil County school. A definite shelf carving and tail in the middle of the body are distinctive characteristics of all of his birds. The bills on his decoys have mandible and nostril carving and take a rather severe dip coming off of the head. The decoys known by him in original paint have wing patterns on their backs. He made canvasback, redhead, blackhead, and black duck decoys.

ENGLISH, DANIEL GLEASON, *1883-1962, FLORENCE, NEW JERSEY —* A maker of finely done, beautifully painted Delaware River decoys, Dan English was born and raised on this river. He followed his father, John English's patterns and design in making birds. He was a wood pattern maker by trade and the quality of his decoys reflects his skill in this occupation. His decoys had nicely rounded bodies with flat bottoms and low contented heads. Made of hollowed two-piece Jersey cedar, they were light in weight and rode the waters of the Delaware very well. His mallards, black ducks, pintails, and widgeon had raised wing carving and detailed feather painting. The diving species, canvasback, redhead, and blackheads, had smooth backs with no raised wing and the same notches cut in the tails that were found on all of his species. He used the lead pad weight typically set far back on the bottom and a leather thong for attaching the anchor line.

FLETCHER, COLUMBUS PAXTON "LUM", *1867-1942, HAVRE DE GRACE, MARYLAND* — Lum Fletcher was born on Swan Creek near the Susquehanna Flats. He spent his early youth hunting and fishing and later guided the sportsmen that came to Havre de Grace on their gunning trips. At one time he worked for the Pennsylvania Railroad which carried many of his patrons into town from the cities to the north. He made decoys only as a sideline and only canvasbacks are known to have been made by Mr. Fletcher. Most of his cans have a higher than normal head and there is mandible and nostril carving in the bill. He made the greater part of his decoys in the late teens and early twenties and sold them for 90 cents each. In some respects his decoys resemble the birds of Sam Barnes.

GIBSON, PAUL, *1902-   , HAVRE DE GRACE, MARYLAND* — Mr. Paul Gibson, a gentleman and fine decoy maker is never too busy for anyone. A visit to his shop is a welcome and friendly experience. He has been making decoys in Havre de Grace since 1915 when he carved his first bird. His production through the early years was limited to hand chopped and hand finished decoys. In the late 1930's he purchased Madison Mitchell's duplicating lathe and continued to make decoys on this device with one man helping him finish and paint them. His pattern is of the Havre de Grace school and is a sturdy, well made, well painted decoy. He has made most species of ducks and Canada geese through the years. Mr. Gibson's production was never great and as such his decoys are very valuable additions to a collection of Susquehanna Flats decoys.

GLEN, CAPTAIN JOHN, *1876-1954, ROCK HALL, MARYLAND* — John "Hump" Glen was born on Piney Neck near Rock Hall, Maryland. He grew up working on the nearby waters of the Chesapeake Bay and farming on the side. He named his place "Decoy Farm."

In 1943 he sold his farm and moved next door to Captain Jesse Urie in Rock Hall, Maryland. Glen had started making decoys for his own use in 1916 and soon after had begun to furnish a number of hunting clubs with their rigs. All of his decoys were hand chopped and finished off with a spokeshave. The knife marks are still visible on his decoys as he never finish sanded them. He is credited with having originally started the use of silhouette goose decoys in Maryland cornfields.

Decoys known by him are Canada geese, canvasbacks, redheads, blackheads, black ducks, mallards, pintail, and baldpates.

All ballast weights were nailed onto the decoys after they were painted by members of the Rock Hall school, therefore to be in original paint, a decoy from this area *must* have an unpainted ballast.

GRAHAM, JOHN B., *1822-1912, CHARLESTOWN MARYLAND* — John Graham was the undertaker in Charlestown and one of five major makers of decoys that came from this small waterfront town on the Northeast River. He was a contemporary of John "Daddy" Holly and Captain Ben Dye and many of his decoys date from the 1840's, 1850's, and 1860's. He apparently made many decoys as a good number of his birds turn up today.

John Graham produced many different styles through the years and some of these are quite different from the others. They all had a very noticeable shelf carving for the head and neck and in most cases were rounder and flatter than the other decoys from the same area. Many of his decoys had mandible carving, but some did not. An unusual characteristic of Graham's decoys is that a greater than normal number of them are branded with the owner's name in the bottom. This reflects the fact that he made a lot of decoys for sale. There are a few of his decoys around with "J. B. GRAHAM" branded in the bottom, indicating decoys made by Graham for his own rig. An early John Graham canvasback with "J. B. GRAHAM" branded in the bottom is a rare and desirable decoy. Species known to have been made by him include canvasback, redhead, blackhead, and black duck. Several teal that display all the Graham characteristics are in local collections and are extremely rare.

John Graham canvasback showing iron keel and brand "J. COUDON" for Joseph Coudon.

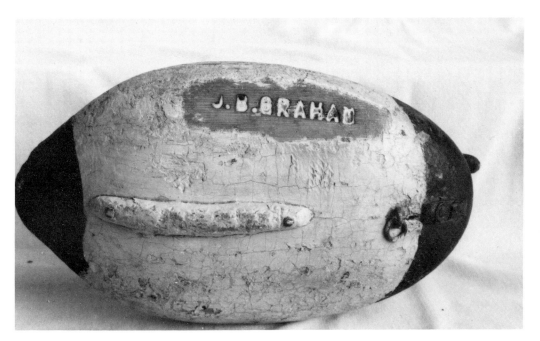

John Graham canvasback from his own gunning rig, branded "J. B. GRAHAM".

GRAY, EDSON, *1891-   , OCEAN VIEW, DELAWARE* — The only decoy maker of note known from the state of Delaware, Edson Gray has spent the greater part of his life on or near the water. He made decoys from the early 1920's through the 1940's. A number of his birds are constructed of hollowed out, two-piece pine or white cedar, while others were made of balsa with a pine head and pine tail insert and a pine keel running along the entire length of the bottom. All of his decoys were made considerably oversized. They were painted very nicely and proved to be attractive and effective working stool. He is known to have made Canada geese, canvasback, redheads, blackheads, mergansers, and black ducks.

HANCOCK, MILES, *1888-1974, CHINCOTEAGUE, VIRGINIA* — Miles Hancock was born a waterman on Chincoteague Island, Virginia in 1888. He harvested the seafood bounty of the area and hunted waterfowl during the season. He began making decoys in the late 1920's for his own use, but soon turned to making them for sale to supplement his waterman's wages. He made decoys for all species that frequent the area, and in later years carved miniatures that were replicas of his full sized hunting decoys. They were all crudely carved and never finish sanded. His paint also appeared primitive and hurried, but it has a nice appeal to it. The knife and rasp marks are very evident through the paint. His decoys were all flat bottomed, different from the other carvers on Chincoteague, and had long slim tails. He died in 1974 after almost fifty years of decoy carving.

HEINEFIELD, AUGUST GEORGE, *1883-1952, ROCK HALL, MARYLAND* — August Heinefield was born in Germany and moved to Baltimore, Maryland in the United States when he was nine years old. Shortly thereafter, his family moved to the Skinners Neck area outside of Rock Hall and Mr. Heinefield grew up learning the trade of carpentry. He never gunned, but began working for John Glen making decoys in 1929. His family estimates that he made no more than several hundred decoys of his own and as such his birds are scarce. His decoys displayed a prominent upswept tail, different from those of John Glen, and all of his heads had very distinct "jaws" carved on the side of the face, again different from those of Mr. Glen. He made canvasbacks, redheads, blackheads, black ducks, baldpates, and a few pintails.

HENDRICKSON, J. EUGENE, *1899-1971, LOWER BANK, NEW JERSEY* — Gene Hendrickson made decoys and sneak boats and worked on the water most of his life. He made traditional Jersey decoys out of hollowed white cedar. His bodies were a little larger than the earlier decoys, and his tails were longer, ending in a point. His heads had detail carving in the bill, and the ballast weights were inletted in the manner of Shourds. Species made by him included Canada goose, brant, canvasback, broadbill, redhead, bufflehead, old squaw, merganser, black duck, mallard, and pintail.

HEVERIN, WILLIAM Y., *1860-1951, CHARLESTOWN, MARYLAND* — Known as "Billy Snakes" along the shores of the Northeast River, where he grew up, Heverin was a fisherman half of the year and a hunter for the other half. He was also a prolific decoy maker who turned out decoys for more than fifty years. Bill Heverin made canvasback, redhead, blackhead, and black duck decoys out of almost any size piece of wood one can imagine, consequently there is a great variation in the size of his birds. Canvasback decoys are known that are close to teal size and black ducks occasionally turn up that are the size of small geese.

A definite shelf carving is evident on all of his decoys as well as a characteristic "smile" carved where the bill joins the cheek. Heverin also made a high tail and low tail model black duck decoy.

HOLLY, JAMES T., *1855-1935, HAVRE DE GRACE, MARYLAND* — "Daddy" Holly's youngest son, Jim, was a decoy maker in his own right. A boatbuilder and craftsman by trade, he made the most seaworthy, yet trim bushwhack boat on the Flats. His boats were said to be unequaled in the water. But he is known today for his classy, sleek black duck decoys. They are long and slender, beautifully painted if found in original paint, and a delight to the collector who owns one. He was an early innovator of the scratch painted black duck and possibly the first on the Chesapeake Bay. He also made canvasback, redhead, blackhead, and mallards. The teal that have often been attributed, in the past, to a Ben Holly were made by Jim Holly.

HOLLY, CAPTAIN JOHN "DADDY", SR., *1818-1892, HAVRE DE GRACE, MARYLAND* — As close as historical research can ascertain, "Daddy" Holly was one of the original designers of the Havre de Grace style of carving sometime around the mid 1830's. He was a market hunter and gunned out of a sink box from the time it was introduced onto the Susquehanna Flats. It appears certain that he made decoys back during this period not only for his own use, but for sale to his fellow hunters.

Early "Daddy" Holly decoys are in collections today that have the "CARROLLS ISLAND" brand in the bottom. This exclusive gun club was formed in the 1830's to shoot canvasback on Carroll's Island at the mouth of the Gunpowder River. John Holly, Sr. made a number of different styles in his decoys through the years, and they are known with shelf carving and also without. Some of his birds have fine detailed carving around the face and bill and tail area, while others are found that are less artistic. Many have the old iron keels and many others the original lead ballast. The few decoys extant by him in original paint show wing and feather patterns that are nicely done. Any decoys by "Daddy" Holly would be a valuable and important addition to anyone's collection. Species known by him are canvasback, redhead, blackhead, teal, and mallard.

HOLLY, WILLIAM, *1845-1923* — HOLLY, JOHN, JR., *1852-1927, HAVRE DE GRACE, MARYLAND* — These two sons of "Daddy" Holly continued the decoy making business started by their father after he passed away in 1892. Their shop was located behind the family home on Alliance Street and here they carried on making canvasback, redheads, and blackheads after the manner of their father. It follows that they would copy their father's patterns and consequently some of their decoys are occasionally confused with "Daddy" Holly's birds. Their decoys are very definitely chunkier and rounder than the smooth looking, slim decoys of their brother James. All of the Holly Family decoys are the class of the Havre de Grace school and are in great demand among knowledgeable decoy collectors.

Unusual iron pad with raised initials "T.J.H." inletted into the bottom of a C-1870 Holly redhead.

Brand "NORTH CAROLINA", a gunning scow on the Flats.

Brand "R. M. VANDIVER" on a Holly canvasback.

Brands "J. F. W." and "E.H.S." on an early C-1865 "DADDY" Holly decoy.

Early Holly hen canvasback in original paint with brand "H. E. & S."

Early Holly decoy with inletted unmarked iron pad and brand "S. G. E."

Bottom of original paint Jim Holly redhead showing unusual inletted lead strip weight and brands "G. B. G." and "D. G. ELLIOTT". Bird was gunned on Currituck Sound.

Original paint Jim Holly canvasback C-1900 showing cast lead, copper name tag from DARBY, PA. and original leather thong.

Early Holly decoy C-1865 showing iron keel and the brand "SUSQUEHANNA", a sister ship to the Reckless.

Jim Holly blackhead C-1890 branded "SPESUTIE I. R. & G. CLUB".

HORNER, NATHAN ROWLEY, *1882-1942, WEST CREEK, NEW JERSEY* —
A true bayman, Rowley Horner made his living clamming, guiding sportsmen from
the cities, building boats, and making decoys. Each collector has his personal preference and many consider Horner's decoys the very finest New Jersey birds. His pure
simplistic style ranks him well ahead of most other makers. His work closely re-
sembles that of the Tuckerton area carvers, but his superior skill is evident in all of
his decoys. His ballast weight was a lead pad with bevelled edge attached after
painting. Decoys known by him are Canada geese, brant, bluebill, redhead, bufflehead.

Rowley Horner beveled edge pad weight fastened with brass screws.

HUDSON, IRA, *1873-1949, CHINCOTEAGUE, VIRGINIA* — Ira Hudson started
making decoys around the turn of the century at his home on Chincoteague. He
made beautifully painted, attractive decoys, many with unusual head positions,
that are in great demand by collectors today. He employed scratch painting extensively and some of his designs in painting are rather elaborate. Almost all of
his decoys had iron upholstery tack eyes. He changed his styles of carving through
the years so that today collectors can build an entire collection out of Ira Hudson
goose decoys. Some of his tails smoothly flowed off of the body, while others
abruptly jutted out as a little paddle type tail. Some were fluted, others were not.
The abrupt tail style has come to be called the "banjo" tail in the collecting world
presumably because of its resemblance to that instrument on his pintails. Some of
his heads sat up over the body on a shelf carving and some sat down in a relief
area that was lower than the back. He carved nostrils, mandibles, and a separation
from the face of the decoy on some bills and others were completely plain with only
the paint indicating the separation. He apparently never weighted his decoys as they
are found with every kind of ballast weight imaginable, many of them typical to
the area where the decoy is found.

Ira Hudson's "hissing head" geese and "crooked neck" brant are rare and
valuable and a joy to the collector who owns one. He is known to have made Canada
geese, brant, canvasback, redhead, blackhead, goldeneye, bufflehead, mallard,
black duck, pintail, widgeon, green wing teal, and red breasted, and hooded
mergansers.

JACKSON, W. SCOTT, *1852-1929, CHARLESTOWN, MARYLAND* — Scott Jackson lived next door to Will Heverin in Charlestown and he and G. W. Barnes were brothers-in-law, but any similarity in their decoys ends when one gets past the common Cecil County characteristics. Scott Jackson's decoys have a classy, racy appearance with an upsweep to the tail and a small shelf carving on which the head and neck rest. Well defined draw knife marks are visible on most of his decoys and this provides a good identification mark in conjunction with his other characteristics. Scott Jackson made canvasback, blackhead, and teal decoys.

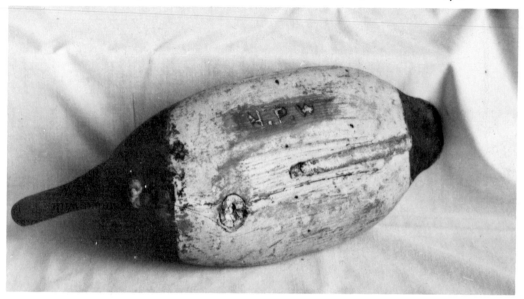

Brand "N. P. W." for Nelson Price Whitaker on a Scott Jackson decoy.

JESTER, DOUGLAS, *1876-1961, CHINCOTEAGUE, VIRGINIA* — A lifelong resident of Chincoteague, Doug Jester was a waterman and decoy maker who never strayed far from his Island home. He hand chopped all of his decoys in the manner of the other decoy makers on Chincoteague. He used white cedar, white pine and cotton wood for his birds and after chopping and a little knife work, they were seldom finished further before painting. Many of his decoys are still available in original paint and the appearance is fairly attractive to the eye of the collector. He sometimes failed to paint eyes on his birds. Almost all of his decoys were long and slim bodied with a shelf for the head and neck to rest upon. He carved nostrils and mandibles in all of his bills. He is known to have made Canada geese, brant, canvasback, redheads, blackheads, buffleheads, goldeneye, mallards, black ducks, pintails, red breasted, and hooded mergansers. In his later years he made miniatures for sale.

JOHNSON, TAYLOR, *1863-1929, POINT PLEASANT, NEW JERSEY* — A bayman all of his life, Johnson made fine hollow cedar New Jersey decoys. He carved a deep hollowed eye groove and a long, slender rounded body. He made redheads, blackheads, black ducks, brant, merganser, and Canada geese.

LOCKARD, HENRY, *1868-1944* — **LOCKARD, GEORGE,** *1866-1931, ELK NECK, MARYLAND* — Henry and George Lockard were both born and raised on Elk Neck, a strip of land called the "mountain shore" by natives of the area. The brothers gunned a sink box out of Cara Cove near the mouth of the Northeast River and made their decoys for their own use. Henry's decoys are usually larger, thicker, and have higher heads than the decoys of George, but both brothers carved half moon nostrils in their bills and this has proved to be a prominent aid to identification. Their tails are usually slightly upswept but still begin down in the middle of the body. Only canvasbacks and redheads are known by the brothers.

LOWE, GILBERT, *1907-*   , *BALTIMORE, MARYLAND* — Mr. Lowe was a wood pattern maker born and raised in Baltimore. He has carved animals for a number of years and naturally made his own decoys to hunt over when he retired and moved to the Eastern Shore. Settling near St. Michaels on the Miles River, Mr. Lowe gunned Canada geese, canvasbacks, and mallards there and on nearby Leeds Creek. He made his mallard decoys flat bottomed and in two pieces out of white cedar telephone poles. He copied the pattern from Eugene Connett's book on duck decoys. His cans were made similar to others made and used at the head of the Bay. Mr. Lowe made one small rig of huge Canada goose decoys with white cedar bodies and mahogany heads.

McGAW, ROBERT F.,   *1879-1958, HAVRE DE GRACE, MARYLAND* — Bob McGaw started making decoys shortly after 1900 and continued to make hand chopped birds until about 1924 when he became the first maker in Havre de Grace to design and have built a duplicating lathe for turning decoy bodies. After each body is turned, one at a time, they must be worked extensively with hand tools before they begin to take shape. To say that these decoys are machine made leaves many collectors with a false impression of the collectibility of these decoys. Bob McGaw's decoys can be consistently identified by the dog boned shaped ballast weight nailed to the decoy with five nails and his paint style. All of his decoys had wing and feather painting on the back and prominent diagonal speculums with slash marks. Species made by him include Canada goose, canvasback, redhead, blackhead, goldeneye, coot, mallard, black duck, baldpate, and pintail.

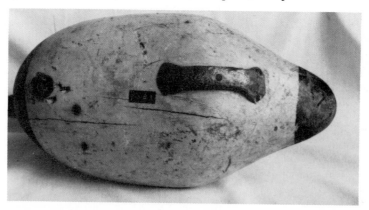

Typical Bob McGaw dog bone shaped lead ballast fastened with 5 nails.

MITCHELL, R. MADISON, *1901-   , HAVRE DE GRACE, MARYLAND* —
Madison Mitchell began making decoys in 1924 by helping Samuel Barnes finish
out his orders for that year. He has been making the Havre de Grace decoy ever
since, in addition to his primary occupation of undertaking. His decoys were completely hand chopped until 1931 when he had a duplicating lathe built and began
turning his bodies on this apparatus. A tremendous amount of hand work is still
put into the decoys as the duplicating lathe does little more than the band saw in
bringing the block of wood to its basic shape. Madison's birds follow closely the
early pattern of the Havre de Grace school with a high upswept tail and no shelf
carving under the head and neck. All of his species are painted with quite a bit of
detail with the marsh ducks being the most elaborately done.

Madison Mitchell's earlier production was mostly Canada geese, canvasback,
redheads, and blackheads. A smaller number of pintails, mallards, blacks, and goldeneye were also turned out during this period. Later he made blue wing and green
wing teal, coot, brant, and bufflehead. Since 1960 he has added most species that
occur in the Atlantic flyway to his output.

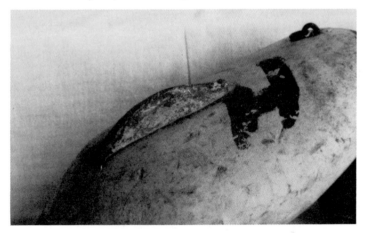

Typical early C-1940 Madison Mitchell cast lead ballast.

PARSONS, EDWARD T., *1856-1937, OXFORD, MARYLAND* — Ed Parsons was
born on the Tred Avon River in Talbot County, Maryland in 1856 and, at the age
of ten, moved with his family to Oxford, Maryland, where he went to work in his
uncle's shipyard. He began his own ship chandlery business in time and, after building a successful business, began making decoys to meet his and other hunter's needs
in the area. He was the only decoy maker who made birds for sale, other than the
Elliot twins, in Talbot County. He made a round, smaller than average decoy and
always cut a concavity under the end of the tail. His ballast weight was melted
lead poured into a one inch hole he bored in the bottom of the decoy. His paint
patterns were simple and effective. He made canvasback, redhead, blackhead, goldeneye, buffleheads, and mergansers.

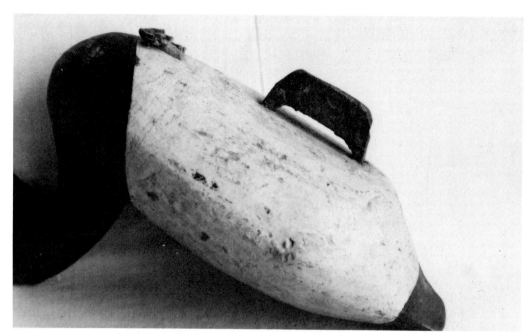

Short iron keel from Talbot County.

PEARSON, EDWIN ERGOOD, *1859-1932, HAVRE DE GRACE, MARYLAND* —
Ed Pearson was born on September 9, 1959 in Havre de Grace, Maryland and
lived there for all of his life. He owned the Kramer Lumberyard on Stokes Street
in the 1920's. He made some of the finest bushwhack boats produced in town and it
is said that his boats were second only to those of James T. Holly. He made canvasback decoys for his own use from 1900 until his death and these are the only species
known to have been made by him. His birds were large, well made, big headed
decoys with a flat top to their bodies and a shelf carving for the head and neck to
sit on. This characteristic is contrary to the general Havre de Grace style. He apparently made some decoys for his friends or for sale as a number of his decoys are
branded "E. PEARSON" in the bottom, indicating birds for use in his own rig,
while others have no brand.

PHILLIPS, EDWARD JAMES, *1901-1964, CAMBRIDGE, MARYLAND* — Ed
Phillips was born in South Dorchester County, Maryland and enjoyed waterfowling
in the nearby waters of Tar Bay at a young age. He started making his decoys in
1920 and he turned out the nicest birds made in Dorchester County. His skill as a
carpenter was reflected in the quality of his decoys. They were well made, sound,
and have withstood the years of rigorous gunning extremely well. All of Mr. Phillips
decoys were made for his own use and he took special pains in applying his paint
patterns. He made Canada geese, canvasback, redhead, blackhead, black duck,
pintail, and widgeon.

PRYOR, LEONARD, *1876-1967, CHESAPEAKE CITY, MARYLAND* — Two distinctly different styles of carving by Leonard Pryor have been defined in recent years. What apparently seems to be his earlier style was possibly made while he lived in the Elk Neck area of Cecil County and could have been influenced by the Lockards who also lived there. These birds have a very definite shelf carving, nostrils similar in style to those of the Lockards, and slightly upswept tails. Many of these birds are found with the earlier iron keels. This style is also found in a sleeper or preener position as were a few Lockard decoys. His other style, possibly made while living in Chesapeake City, features a smooth, sleek, finely done decoy with no shelf carving and smaller nostrils. Some marsh species were done in this style and some of these birds were hollow, in two pieces, and had raised wing carving similar to the Delaware River style. Species known in the first model are canvasback only. The second style includes canvasback, blackhead, black duck and pintail.

SHOURDS, HARRY MITCHELL, *1889-1944, OCEAN CITY, NEW JERSEY* — Harry Mitchell Shourds made decoys in the manner of his father, Harry Van Knukson Shourds, and they are very similar in style, paint, and design. The heads on Mitchell Shourds decoys are smaller and have less cheek than those of his father. They are made of the same Jersey white cedar, in two pieces and hollowed out. They also have the same inletted poured lead ballast weight. He carved nostrils and mandibles in his bills as did his father. With all of the similarities and closeness of design, the decoys of these two famous Jersey makers are still easily distinguishable to the practiced eye. Harry M. Shourds made all of the same species in decoys that his father did.

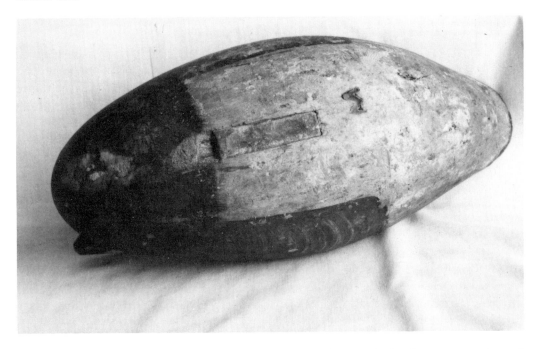

Harry Shourds brant showing poured lead weight, typical of a Harry Shourds decoy.

"Dugout-"Joe King, Manahawkin, New Jersey body showing chisel gouge marks and raised area in bottom for inletted poured lead.

SHOURDS, HARRY V., *1871-1920, TUCKERTON, NEW JERSEY* — Harry Shourds made very fine hollow, simply styled decoys that many consider among the finest of New Jersey Coast decoys. He was a house painter and later a decoy maker by trade. His birds were standard sized as were almost all Jersey decoys, and dug out by hand to create a very light in weight decoy. His ballast weight was melted lead poured into an inlet approximately 3" x ¾" cut into the bottom center of the decoy. His work is known in the following species: Canada goose, brant, bluebill, redhead, bufflehead, goldeneye, red breasted merganser, old squaw, black duck, and pintail.

SPRAGUE, CHRIS, *1887-   , BEACH HAVEN, NEW JERSEY* — Chris Sprague was in law enforcement work in his younger years, but turned to decoy making, gunning, and guiding in the 1930's as his full-time work. His decoys are hollow two-piece white cedar and are finely carved. He worked in conjunction with Rowley Horner and Ellis Parker in 1935 to make the famous rig mentioned in Bill Mackey's book *American Bird Decoys*. Together they made an almost unparalleled New Jersey decoy. Chris was known to have made Canada geese, brant, bluebills, goldeneyes, black ducks, mallards, and mergansers.

TRAVERS, JOSIAH FRANKLIN, *1900-1965, VIENNA, MARYLAND* — Another Dorchester County maker who carved a desirable and attractive decoy for the collector of today. He was raised on the Nanticoke River which runs past Vienna, Maryland, where he grew up. A lot of effort was put into the carving and painting of Uncle Joe's decoys as evidenced by the fine examples found in local collections. His wooden decoys had a curious "turtle back" appearance and the head was usually very slender and on the small side in proportion to the body. He used iron upholstery tacks for eyes and worked a number of details into his bills including mandible carving and a nail on the end of the bill. Joe Travers made cork black duck and Canada goose decoys. They had pine heads and the blacks had pine bottom boards. A lot of carving of the wing outline and shoulder gouge shows up on the cork decoys and a considerable amount of feathering detail on the black duck heads is employed. A screen door spring runs through a sleeve in the cork goose body and holds the head in place. A rocking motion is imparted by the action of the waves on the floating decoy. Joe Travers also made wooden canvasback, blackheads, mallard, and widgeon.

TRUEX, RHODES, *Died 1934, ATLANTIC CITY, NEW JERSEY* — Rhodes Truex worked for the State of New Jersey as a bridge tender and made decoys for sale to others. His decoys were typical Jersey hollowed white cedar with a pad type ballast of lead. His eyes were impressed in the soft cedar and painted. There is detail carving in the bill in the form of nostrils and some of his decoys were scratch painted. He made Canada geese, brant, broadbill, goldeneye, red breasted merganser, and black duck.

TYLER, LLOYD J., *1898-1971, CRISFIELD, MARYLAND* — Lloyd Tyler made his first decoy in 1910 in Crisfield, Maryland where he was born and raised. He lived most of his life across the street from the famous Ward brothers and some similarity to their work in his style is evident. Lloyd knew what a duck looked like and he realistically captured that look in the attitude and paint pattern on his decoys. They were crude but effective. He never finished the decoy with more than a hatchet or rasp and these marks are bold on his work. All of his birds were flat bottomed as was the common Crisfield style. He is known to have made Canada geese and most all of the species of ducks that frequented the Crisfield area.

URIE, CAPTAIN JESSE, *1901-1978, ROCK HALL, MARYLAND* — Captain Jesse was born in Rock Hall, Maryland and lived in this waterfront fishing village on the Chesapeake Bay for most of his life. He was a fisherman and owned several party boats with which he ran charter fishing trips through the years. He began making decoys with John Glen when Glen moved next door in 1943 and continued making them until the day he passed away in 1978. All of his decoys were hand chopped until about 1955 when he purchased a duplicating lathe and began turning his bodies on this machine. He quit making gunning stool in 1968 and turned full-time to producing the miniatures that were identical in style and paint to his full sized birds.

Capt. Jesse's decoys have wide, sturdy bills that are a distinctive trademark. There is a very definite "flat" to the breast on both his hand chopped and lathe turned birds, because he seldom rounded fully the cut off where the block was cut to its proper length.

All of the decoys of Capt. Jesse Urie, Capt. John Glen, and August Heinefield had fully painted feather and wing patterns on the back.

Capt. Urie made Canada geese, canvasback, redhead, blackhead, goldeneye, black duck, mallard, pintail, and baldpate. He also made an oversized black duck and canvasback model.

WARD, LEM, *1896-   — STEVE 1895-1976, CRISFIELD, MARYLAND* — Lem and Steve Ward were born on the lower Eastern Shore of Maryland in Crisfield, one of the largest seafood centers in the country. Their father, L. Travis Ward, Sr., was a barber, a waterman, and a decoy maker and the boys followed naturally in his stead. Acknowledged as the master decoy makers in the mid-Atlantic region, Lem and Steve turned out the typical flat bottomed, wide hipped Crisfield decoy from 1918 through the 1950's. The carving, attitude, and paint jobs on their working birds is considered by many to have been unsurpassed during the time they worked. Their style has varied through the years so that they have produced a number of significantly different designs, all of them extremely appealing to the collector of today. They made decoys for most species of ducks and Canada geese.

WATSON, DAVE "UMBRELLA", *Died 1938, CHINCOTEAGUE, VIRGINIA* — Little information is known of this carver from Chincoteague Island, but his beautifully carved and painted decoys that exist today speak for themselves. Coming from Chincoteague, conjecture leads one to figure Dave Watson was a waterman as so many of his contemporaries, but his peers in decoy making were few. He made a hollow, two-piece wooden decoy whose profile suggests a New Jersey coast influence. However, he carved a raised wing on all of his duck, goose, and brant decoys which is different not only from Jersey birds, but also the typical Virginia decoy. Each bird displays a brow carving over the eyes which often gives the appearance of an angry expression to the decoy and is a good aid to identification. His painting was exquisitely done in a detailed manner. He is known to have made Canada goose, canvasback, brant, blackduck, and pintail.

WILLIAMS, JOHN, *1857-1937, CEDAR ISLAND, VIRGINIA* — John Williams is known today for his fantastic swan decoys made before 1900 and his diminutive, but fascinating tiny ruddy ducks. Both birds were commonly hunted in the late nineteenth century on Back Bay and Currituck Sound and some of the better decoys that have turned up that were made for these species are found in this area. Mr. Williams was a guide at Cedar Island in later years and undoubtably hunted the "dollar duck", as the ruddy was known, for the market in his younger days. This would account for his rig of ruddies. He made decoys for his own use only and consequently few are left today that remain uncollected. Species other than ruddy duck and swan were surely made by Williams but are unknown as of this writing.

A typical selection of lead anchor weights used on the Susquehanna Flats.

Typical iron anchor weights used in the Mid-Atlantic Region, showing the number of various designs. The iron weight on the right forefront and the third from the left in the lower row are painted yellow to simulate corn under the anchored decoys.

CHAPTER 8

Collecting, Restoration and Values

Collecting wooden decoys has been enjoying a tremendous upsurge in growth in recent years and a few guidelines on the current trends in collecting might be helpful to the individual contemplating a move in the direction of decoys.

It is very difficult to advise someone on what to collect and how to go about collecting it. Suggestions can be made, but they oftentimes fall on deaf ears. It seems that almost all new collectors are so eager to gather a bunch of decoys around them immediately that they throw all caution and wisdom to the winds and swoop down on every decoy they can find for under $30 with their money waving wildly in their fist. At most times it would be far better to forego those six or eight decoys for $200 and wisely purchase one decoy that is worthwhile. Of course at this point, we run into one other major consideration which, to my way of thinking, should be our primary objective with anything which we collect — that is, that a collector should buy what he likes! If you see a decoy for $25 that really appeals to your collecting sense, then buy it. Never mind that the dealer has said that the bird will only increase in value by 10% next year whereas the $200 bird might increase ten times that much. Buy it if you really like it. After all you're the only one that has to live with your purchase. As you become more experienced and knowledgable your tastes might change or you may realize that in your early years of collecting you made a mistake in purchasing a certain bird. There will be time enough to pass it on in a deal to another new collector who feels exactly about that decoy as you did years before.

Your collecting now has a purpose or direction to it, you have decided that you would like to collect Delaware River decoys, or Chesapeake Bay decoys, or birds by Harry Shourds or Ira Hudson, or canvasbacks, or Canada geese or just black ducks from the Susquehanna Flats. Any number of avenues are open for your approach and selecting one of these specific paths will be your first step toward building an important and valuable collection.

Your next step is recognizing a reputable, knowledgable dealer in decoys that you can trust, and by working with that dealer or dealers, and attending the numerous shows that abound, and talking to other collectors, and visiting their collections, and reading your books on decoys, you will see your collection begin to grow.

If you have decided to collect decoys by Madison Mitchell, then you should be constantly seeking all species of decoys by him. Don't pass up the opportunity to look at and handle or learn about other decoys, especially when visiting well known collections, but do alert your dealer and collector friends to that which you are seeking so that they may be on the lookout for something good for you. And ask about at all of the shows which you attend for those decoys in which you are interested. You should try to obtain the oldest documented examples and the ones in the best original condition for each species and in this manner you can constantly upgrade your collection. Let the price fall where it may. Only you are aware of what you can afford and the price of any decoy is relative to a multitude of conditions. What one man can afford and will readily pay, another man may find outrageous. A decoy in original mint condition in the eyes of one collector may only rate as good to another. If one enthusiast needs only a pair of pre-1940 Madison Mitchell pintails to complete his marsh duck species, he may be willing to pay $500, while another man who already has two pairs or will settle for any before 1955 may only be willing to pay half that amount. Many times only an exorbitant offer on the part of some anxious buyer will persuade the owner to sell the decoys in question. *The prices listed at the end of this chapter are only a listing of prices realized at recent sales and should not be regarded as a price guid.* Please make note of the fact that most of these prices are at least a year old as of this writing and will be even more out of date by the time this book is published. In light of these facts, this listing could hardly be considered more than a casual reference guide.

Restoration of a decoy is another topic under much controversial discussion today and no matter what anyone may say, novice or expert, the topic boils down very simply to a matter of personal preference. There are more than enough highly skilled, accomplished restoration experts today that can transform a missing bill into a completely undetectable repair. And who is to tell a collector that he must not or should not replace a missing bill or a chipped tail or tighten a cracked neck. One person may believe that a 1936 Ward canvasback with a part of its small tail chipped out should be left as it is, because it pleases him in that condition, while another collector might feel a lot better about the bird if its tail was fully restored. It is strictly a matter of personal opinion and that collector should do as he feels is proper, not what some almighty expert tries to make him believe is the correct thing to do.

Now if a dealer restores or has restored any part of a decoy, be it a part of the bird or the paint on the bird, then it should be noted and sold as a restored bird. Many people will argue that this is fine until the decoy moves on to a third party and what was originally sold as a restored decoy is now sold as all original. This argument is sound and is granted, but it still raises the question of the position of the original owner who was dissatisfied with the decoy in its unrestored condition. It is a matter of ethics and downright honesty that cannot be solved with any more discussion here.

In a recent publication, *Martha's Vineyard Decoys,* Mr. Stanley Murphy, the author, condones stripping completely the many old coats of paint from a bird and revealing fully the sculptural art form. His writing makes very clear the fact that his birds in this condition pleased him and that, my friends, is what is important. This collector does not agree with the man, but I certainly can't criticize him for his preference. Many decoys in my collection have been cleaned to as close to the first coat of paint as possible and much bare wood is showing in some cases, but as Mr. Murphy agrees, I value them no less than others in full paint. One other point about paint that I would like to touch upon — a decoy repainted by the maker is *not* in its original paint. A bird repainted one or a number of times by its maker will command a slightly higher value than if it was repainted by another, but it will not bring the same value as a decoy in its original or first coat of paint.

One last item, all of this hullabaloo raised about wax or oil is just that, a lot of hullaballoo. Wax applied to a decoy by its owner is again, that owner's personal preference, and the idea circulating in the decoy world today that wax or oil will harm the intrinsic value of a decoy is absurd. A decoy is made of wood and paint and wax or oil can enhance, feed, and help to preserve the wood and paint, and if an owner of a collection of decoys desires to apply a coat of wax or a coat of oil and turpentine to his birds, then why should anyone try to tell him what he should or should not do. I have been applying a light coat of linseed oil, turpentine, and vinegar to my decoys for a number of years and recommend it if anyone feels the need to put something on their birds.

In conclusion, while we are speaking of value and conditions that affect it, it should be noted that very few if any old time decoy makers signed their decoys. Innumerable times the first question posed by the unenlightened will be "Is it signed?" A couple of makers, out of the region discussed in this book, did mark or brand the decoys they made but not consistently enough to be a sure fire identification aid. A number of makers have signed their decoys in subsequent years as they were requested by collectors who returned to them with their old decoys and perhaps this is where the notion came from that the only really good decoy is a signed decoy. This, of course, is far from being true and it is hoped that this information will help to educate the uninformed.

SUSQUEHANNA FLATS

CARROLL "WALLY" ALGARD	$ 35—250.00
CHARLES N. BARNARD	50—500.00
THOMAS BARNARD	45—200.00
GEORGE "WASH" BARNES	35—500.00
SAMUEL BARNES	28—300.00
TAYLOR BOYD	35—200.00
JIM CURRIER	30—150.00
HENRY DAVIS	35— 95.00
BEN DYE	55—650.00
JOSEPH DYE	50—600.00
COLUMBUS "LUM" FLETCHER	35—100.00
PAUL GIBSON	25—100.00
JOHN B. GRAHAM	40—350.00
WILLIAM HEVERIN	45—250.00
JOHN "DADDY" HOLLY	55—650.00
JAMES HOLLY	45—650.00
JOHN JR. AND WILLIAM HOLLY	45—300.00
SCOTT JACKSON	65—175.00
HARRY JOBES	25— 95.00
GEORGE LOCKARD	38—150.00
HENRY LOCKARD	50—300.00
ROBERT F. McGAW	25—250.00
R. MADISON MITCHELL	25—175.00
ED PEARSON	40—100.00
JIM PIERCE	25— 85.00
LEONARD PRYOR	45—150.00
MILTON WATSON	35—150.00
CHARLES WILSON	150—650.00

H.A. FLECKENSTEIN JR.

NEW JERSEY COAST

L. APPLEGATE	$ 50—250.00
LOU BARKELOW	45—200.00
JAKE BARRETT	65—500.00
EUGENE BIRDSAW	45—200.00
JESSE BIRDSAW	55—400.00
J. W. BOWEN	35—200.00
BILL BROWN	35—350.00
RUBEN CORLIES	25—200.00
LOU CRANMER	25—600.00
JOHN DORSETT	35—275.00
AMOS DOUGHTY	65—200.00
MARK ENGLISH	65—650.00
SAM FORSYTH	45—250.00
PERCY GANT	45—300.00
HENRY GRANT	45—500.00
STANLEY GRANT	35—250.00
WILLIAM HALL	35—175.00
BILL HAMMILL	35—200.00
GENE HENDRICKSON	35—150.00
ROWLEY HORNER	65—500.00
JOHN INMAN	35—200.00
TAYLOR JOHNSON	35—450.00
WILLIS JOHNSON	35—250.00
MARK KEAR	65—450.00
HENRY KILPATRICK	55—375.00
JOE KING	65—175.00
ROY MAXWELL	75—225.00
CHARLES McCOY	35—400.00
ELLIS PARKER	45—350.00
LLOYD PARKER	65—750.00
LIBERTY PRICE	?
JOHN ROBERTS	75—195.00
BRADFORD SALMON	65—215.00
HARRY M. SHOURDS	55—650.00
HARRY V. SHOURDS	65—1000.00
CHRIS SPRAGUE	65—750.00
RHODES TRUEX	45—250.00
JOHN UPDIKE	35—175.00

DELAWARE RIVER

CHARLES ALLEN	$ 75–250.00
RICHARD ANDERSON	65–200.00
SAM ARCHER	100–350.00
J. BAKER	55–150.00
COOPER BERKLEY	65–275.00
CHARLES BLACK	75–300.00
JOHN BLAIR	150–1000.00
WALTER BUSH	100–300.00
JOHN DAWSON	100–1675.00
DAN ENGLISH	65–250.00
JACK ENGLISH	65–250.00
JOHN ENGLISH	100–450.00
TOM FITZPATRICK	45–155.00
PAUL GREEN	65–210.00
JOHN HEISLER	75–250.00
CHARLES HUFF	55–200.00
JOE KING	65–250.00
CLARK MADIERI	55–300.00
REGINALD MARTER	45–200.00
LAWRENCE MC GLAUGHLIN	45–275.00
JOHN MC GLOUGHLIN	55–350.00
WILLIAM QUINN	65–425.00
AL REITZ	55–265.00

CHESAPEAKE BAY

DON BRIDDELL .... $ 35—100.00
DAN BROWN .... 35—175.00
CHARLES BRYAN .... 25—100.00
JIM COCKEY .... 35—125.00
BILL AND CHANK ELLIOTT .... 25— 75.00
JOHN GLEN .... 35—200.00
AUGUST HEINEFIELD .... 35—200.00
CHARLES JOINER .... 25—175.00
PHIL KEMP .... 25—150.00
OLIVER LAWSON .... 35—200.00
ED PARSONS .... 45—400.00
TOM PARSONS .... 55—400.00
ED PHILLIPS .... 65—300.00
JOHN SMITH .... 25—125.00
LLOYD STERLING .... 55—250.00
WILL STERLING .... 55—250.00
ALEX TRAVERS .... 25—195.00
JOSIAH TRAVERS .... 25—300.00
LLOYD TYLER .... 25—600.00
JESSE URIE .... 25—200.00
JOHN VICKERS .... 35—550.00
LEM AND STEVE WARD .... 100—3500.00

H.A. FLECKENSTEIN JR. '74

VIRGINIA AND NORTH CAROLINA

CHARLES BIRCH . . . .$ 40–4000.00
BULL FAMILY. 25–200.00
NED BURGESS 25–300.00
COBB FAMILY. 95–2000.00
JOSEPH CRUMB 65–375.00
LEE AND LEM DUDLEY. 300–2000.00
EDSON GRAY 35–700.00
MILES HANCOCK 35–300.00
IRA HUDSON. 45–1800.00
CHARLES JESTER 35–250.00
DOUG JESTER. 35–300.00
DAVE WATSON. 65–1000.00
JOHN WILLIAMS. 100–3000.00

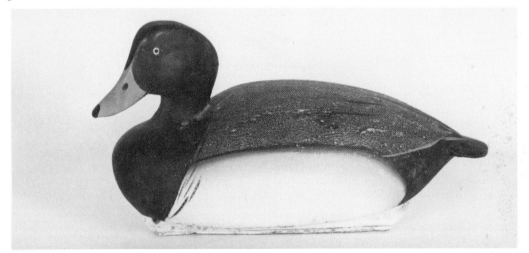

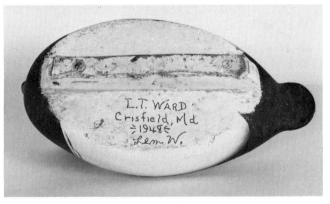

BOOKS SUGGESTED FOR FURTHER READING ON DECOYS

Barber, Joel — *Wild Fowl Decoys* — originally published 1934 by Windward House. Available now — Dover Publications, 1954 — in print.

Berkey, Barry — *Pioneer Decoy Carvers* — 1977, Tidewater Publishers — Available now — in print.

Buckwalter, Harold R. — *Susquehanna River Decoys* — 1978, Harold Buckwalter — Available now — in print.

Cheever, Byron — *Mason Decoys* — 1974, Hillcrest Publications — Available now — in print.

Cheever, Byron, editor — *North American Decoys* — Quarterly Periodical — Available now — in print.

Colio, Quintina — *American Decoys* — 1972, Science Press — Available now — in print.

Earnest, Adele — *The Art of The Decoy* — originally 1965 by Clarkson N. Potter — Available now, Bramhall House — in print.

Frank, Charles W. — *Louisiana Duck Decoys* — 1975, Charles W. Frank — Available now — in print.

Johnsgard, Paul A., editor — *The Bird Decoy* — 1976, University of Nebraska Press — Available now — in print.

Mackey, William — *American Bird Decoys* — originally 1965 by Dutton — Available now, Schiffer Limited — 1979 — in print.

McKinney, J. Evans — *Decoys of the Susquehanna Flats* — 1978, Holly Press — Available now — in print.

Murphy, Stanley — *Martha's Vineyard Decoys* — 1978 — David R. Godine — Available now — in print.

North American Decoys — *Ward Bros.* — no date — North American Decoys — Available now — in print.

Parmalee and Loomis — *Decoys and Decoy Carvers of Illinois* — 1969, Northern Illinois University Press — Out of print.

Reed, M. Clarke, editor — *Decoy World* — Quarterly periodical — Available now — in print.

Richardson, R. H., editor — *Chesapeake Bay Decoys* — 1973, Crow Haven Publishers — Available on the rare book market — Out of print.

Sorenson, Harold D. — *Decoy Collector's Guide* — 1963-1979. Harold D. Sorenson — Available now — in print.

Starr, George Ross, Jr. — *Decoys of the Atlantic Flyway* — 1974, Winchester Press — Available now — in print.

Walsh, Harry — *The Outlaw Gunner* — 1971, Tidewater Publishers — Available now — in print.

Walsh, Roy — *Gunning the Chesapeake* — 1961, Tidewater Publishers — Available now — in print.

Webster and Kehoe, David and William — *Decoys at Shelburne Museum* — originally 1961, Shelburne Museum — Available now 1971, Shelburne Museum — in print.

PICTURE CREDITS

John Hillman, 21, 22, 23, 24, 25, 26, 27, 28, 29, 30, 31, 33, 34, 35, 36, 37, 38, 39, 41, 42, 43, 46, 47, 48, 49, 51, 52, 53, 54, 55, 58, 59, 60, 61, 62, 63, 64, 65, 66, 67, 68, 69, 70, 71, 72, 73, 74, 75, 76, 77, 78, 85, 86, 140, 141, 144; Larry Lambert, 32, 44, 45, 118, 152, 175, 176, 177 (bottom), 195, 196, 199, 213, 220, 223 (top), 225, 226, 228 (top); Old Print Shop, New York City, 122 (bottom), 154 (bottom), 166 (bottom), 181 (bottom), 228 (bottom); Refuge Waterfowl Museum, Chincoteague, Virginia, 223 (bottom), 224; Robert H. Richardson, 40, 87, 108, 132, 133, 136, 145, 148, 150, 153, 156 (bottom), 157 (bottom), 160, 162, 163, 164, 165, 167, 168, 169, 170, 172, 173, 174, 178, 179, 180, 181 (top), 182, 183, 184, 185, 186, 187, 194, 198, 202, 203, 204, 205, 207, 209, 210, 211, 212, 216, 219, 222 (bottom); George Reiger, 218 (bottom); John Sullivan, 177 (top); Herbert Schiffer Antiques, 120 (bottom), 136, 146, 151 (top), 158 (bottom), 231; Rick and June Fish, 120 (top); Henry A. Fleckenstein Jr., 15, 50, 84, 86 (bottom), 88, 89, 90, 91, 92, 93, 94, 95, 96, 97, 98, 99, 100, 102, 103, 104, 105, 106, 107, 109, 110, 111, 112, 113, 114, 115, 116, 117, 121, 122 (top), 123, 124, 125, 126, 127, 128, 129, 130, 131, 134, 135, 136, 137, 138, 145, 147, 149, 151 (bottom), 154 (top), 155, 156 (top), 157 (top), 158 (top), 159, 161, 166 (top), 192, 193, 201, 206, 208, 222 (top), 234, 236, 237, 239, 240, 241, 242, 243, 244, 245, 246, 247, 248, 249, 252; Kenny and Donna Gleason, 20, 218 (top); William Walsh, 119, 197, 200, 214, 215, 217, 221, 227.

H.A. FLECKENSTEIN JR.

BIBLIOGRAPHY

American Bird Decoys — William Mackey — E. P. Dutton — 1965.

The American Sportsman — Elisha J. Lewis, M.D. — Philadelphia — 1855.

The Art of the Decoy — Adele Earnest — Clarkson N. Potter — 1965.

Audubon Magazine — January 1976 — Vol. 78, No. 1 — "Fare Thee Well Currituck Banks" — pgs. 22-35.

Barnegat Ways — A. P. Richardson — The Century Co. — New York — 1931.

The Bay and River, Delaware — David Budlong Tyler — Cornell Maritime Press — 1955.

Cabinet of Natural History and American Rural Sports — J. J. Sharpless, M.D. — Philadelphia — 1830, 1832, 1833 — 3 volumes.

Chesapeake Bay Decoys — R. H. Richardson, editor — Crow Haven Publishers — 1973.

Decoy Collectors Guide — Hal Sorenson, editor — 1963-1979.

Decoy World Magazine — F. Kreiser, Salisbury, Maryland and M. Clarke Reed, Jr., Trappe, Maryland — 1974-1979.

Decoys of the Atlantic Flyway — George Ross Starr, Jr. — Winchester Press — 1974.

Hunting and Shooting of North America — edited by Wm. T. Porter, Esq. — Philadelphia — 1846.

Krider's Sporting Anecdotes — edited by H. Milnor Klapp — Philadelphia — 1853.

The Lure of Long Beach — Long Beach Island, New Jersey — Charles Edgar Nash — Long Beach Board of Trade — 1936.

North American Decoys Magazine — Hillcrest Publications — Spanish Fork, Utah — 1967-1979.

Scribner's Monthly Magazine — November 1877, Vol. XV, No. 1 — "Canvasback and Terrapin", pgs. 1-13.

Sunday Magazine — The Sun, Baltimore, Maryland — "A Carver of Ducks for 38 years, R. Madison Mitchell" — John Dorsey — December 2, 1962 — pgs. 18, 19.

Toller Trader Magazine — Murray Mitterhoff, Springfield, New Jersey — 1971-1973.

Wild Fowl Decoys — Joel Barber — Windward House — 1934.

Wildlife in North Carolina Magazine — "North Carolina Decoys and Their Makers", James S. Lewis, Jr. — November 1977 — February 1978 — Parts 1-4.

INDEX

A

Aberdeen, Maryland, 150
Absecon, New Jersey, 25, 26, 28, 35, 37, 38, 43, 52, 55
Aiken, Maryland, 138
Algard, Carroll "Wally", 229
  canvasback decoy, 97, 104, 135
Allen, Charles, canvasback decoy, 76
American Bird Decoys, 233, 249
American Revolution, 13
American Sportsman, The, 80
Anchor, mooring, 82
Anderson, Richard, black duck decoy, 63
Applegate family, red breasted merganser decoy, 24
Archer, Sam, red breasted merganser decoy, 68
Art of the Decoy, The, 13
Atlantic City, New Jersey, 42, 55, 250
Audubon, J.J., 122, 154, 166, 181, 228

B

Back Bay, Virginia, 190, 251
Back River, 16
Baird, 80
Baker, J., black duck decoy, 60
Ballance family, 233
Ballast Weights, New Jersey, 19, 20
Baltimore, 14, 80, 146, 245
"Banjo Tail" Hudson decoy, 194, 195
Barber, Joel, 13, 14, 57
Barkelow, Lou, scaup decoy, 36
Barnard, Charles Nelson, viii, 134, 229
  canvasback decoy, 121, 134
  redhead decoy, 109
Barnegat Bay, 19
Barnegat, New Jersey, 14, 25, 30, 31, 36, 38, 39, 40, 42, 43, 46, 50, 52, 53, 54, 230
Barnes, George Washington, 229, 244
  black duck decoy, 129
  blue wing teal decoy, 84
  canvasback decoy, 128
Barnes, Samuel T., xii, 14, 79, 83, 230, 246
  black duck decoy, 111
  Canada goose decoy, 125
  canvasback decoy, 98, 104, 112, 121, 137
  redhead decoy, 112
  scaup decoy, 91

Barrett, Jake,
  bufflehead decoy, 27
  goldeneye decoy, 77
Battery shooting, 14, 79
Bay Head, New Jersey, 49
Bayville, New Jersey, 24
Beach Haven, New Jersey, 32, 49, 51, 249
Bell, Al, 146
"Ben Holly", 86
Berkley, Cooper, scaup decoy, 78
Betterton, Maryland, 146, 147, 150
Birch, Charles, 189, 190
  black duck decoy, 196, 212, 221
  brant, 207
  Canada goose decoy, 211, 214
  goldeneye decoy, 212
  pintail decoy, 212
  scaup decoy, 212, 213
  swan decoy, 216
Birdsall, Eugene, redhead decoy, 36
Birdsall, Jesse, 230
  black duck decoy, 21
  Canada goose decoy, 53
  goldeneye decoy, 30
Bishop's Head Gun Club, 179
Blair decoys, 59, 62, 65, 141
Blair, John, 57, 83, 230
  pintail decoy, 59, 65, 145
Bob-O-Del Club, 186, 201
Bohemia River, 16
Boice, Harry, 22
Bon Air Farm, xi
Bonnett Club, 31
Bordentown, New Jersey, 60, 62, 63, 68, 70, 71, 74
Bowen, J.W.,
  black duck decoy, 42
  Canada goose decoy, 55
Boyd, Charles, 80
Boyd, Taylor, 230
  black duck decoy, 100
  canvasback decoy, 104
  redhead decoy, 100
Brady, Walter, Canada goose decoy, 215
Brands,
  D.G. ELLIOTT, 241
  E.H.S., 240
  E. PEARSON, 247
  G.A.E., 110
  G.B.G., 241
  H.E. & S., 241
  J.B. GRAHAM, 236
  J. COUDON, 236

  J.F.W., 240
  J. PUSEY, 121
  NORTH CAROLINA, 240
  N.P.W., 244
  R.M. VANDIVER, 113, 240
  S.G.E., 241
  SPESUTIE I.R. & G. CLUB, 242
  SUSQUEHANNA, 242
Brothers, Robert, redhead decoy, 225
Brown, Bill, black duck decoy, 39
Bryan, Charles, 146
  mallard decoy, 150
Budd, Judson, hooded merganser decoy, 160
Bull family, 190
Burgess, Ned, 191, 231
  canvasback decoy, 226
Bush River, 16, 80
Bush, Walter, black duck decoy, 149
Bushwhacking, 16

C

Cabinet of Natural History, 139
Cabot, Edward, green wing teal decoy, 119
Cambridge, Maryland, 92, 145, 149, 154, 156, 163, 247
Cane, Cliff, scaup decoy, 32
Cantwell, Robert, 13
Canvasback, 13
Cape Charles, Virginia, 189
Cape May, New Jersey, 73
Cara Cove, 245
Carpenter's Point, Maryland, 84, 128, 129, 229
"Carroll's Island" brand, 80, 239
Castle Haven Gun Club, 155
Cecil County, Maryland, 80, 81, 85, 129, 229, 230, 232, 233, 234
Cedar Island, Virginia, 224, 251
Chapin, Henry Dwight, 80
Charlestown, Maryland, 14, 79, 81, 84, 85, 98, 99, 103, 104, 106, 107, 108, 109, 110, 113, 123, 128, 135, 149, 229, 236, 238, 243
Chesapeake Bay, ix, x, 14, 16, 79, 81, 139, 142, 143
Chesapeake City, Maryland, 105, 110, 123, 248
Chester River, ix, x, 16
Chincoteague, Virginia, 14, 83, 145, 160, 183, 186, 192, 193, 194, 195, 197, 198, 199, 200-215, 217, 218, 220, 237, 243, 244, 251

Choptank, Maryland, 142
Choptank River, ix, 16, 154
Church's Island, North Carolina, 225, 226, 227, 231
"Cleveland" canvasback decoy, 109, 128
Cobb, Elkenah, black duck decoy, 217
Cobb family, 189, 190, 231
    brant decoy, 136, 145, 219
Cobb Island, Virginia, 99, 136, 145, 217, 218, 219, 220
Cobb, Nathan, Jr., brant decoy, 218, 220
Cockey, Jim, 232
Columbia, Pennsylvania, 124
Cook's Point, 142
Cork decoys, 111, 125, 126, 161
Coudon, Joseph,
    black duck decoy, 138
    Canada goose decoy, 138
Cranmer, Lou, brant decoy, 47
Creighton, Clarence Hix, red breasted merganser decoy, 160
Crisfield, Maryland, 132, 133, 136, 141 142, 165-180, 182-186, 250, 251
Croyden, Pennsylvania, 64, 76
Crumb, Joseph H., Sr., Canada goose decoy, 214, 232
Currier, James, 83, 134, 232
    black duck, 94
    canvasback decoy, 96, 97
    redhead decoy, 96
    scaup decoy, 96
Currituck Sound, North Carolina, 14, 190, 251

D

Daisey, Delbert "Cigar", scaup decoy, 195
Davis, Ben, 80
Davis, Henry, canvasback wing duck, wooden, 114, 137
Dawson, John, 233
    baldpate decoy, 67
    black duck decoy, 67
    canvasback decoy, 66, 145
    mallard decoy, 66
    pintail decoy, 67, 145
    red breasted merganser decoy, 66, 145
    redhead decoy, 67, 145
Delanco, New Jersey, 60, 63, 64, 68, 71, 77, 141
Delaware River, 13, 57, 59, 79, 83, 141, 233
Detroit, Michigan, 24, 43
Devil's Island, 80
Dize, John, 190
Dodge Decoy Co. scaup decoy, 43
Donahue, 80

Dorchester County, Maryland, 156, 158, 159, 160, 164, 183, 187, 216
Dorsett, John, Canada goose decoy, 54
Doughty, Amos, red breasted merganser decoy, 25
Doughty family scaup, 221
Duck Island, New Jersey, 66, 67, 233
Duck, North Carolina, 225
Dudley, Lee and Lem, 191
    Canada goose decoy, 223
    canvasback decoy, 223
    scaup decoy, 221
"Dugout" as used on the Flats, 80
"Dugout" decoy, 19
Dye, Captain Ben, vi, 79, 82, 230, 234, 236
    black duck decoy, 101
    blue wing teal decoy, 84, 101
    canvasback decoy, 100, 101, 122, 136, 137
    redhead decoy, 92, 127
    scaup decoy, 100
Dye, Joseph, 234
    black duck decoy, 101
    canvasback decoy, 98, 109
    redhead decoy, 100, 127
    scaup decoy, 100, 101, 127

E

Earnest, Adele, 13, 119
Eastern Neck Island, 142
Eastern Shore, Maryland, ix, x
Eastern shore of Virginia, 189
East New Market, Maryland, ix, xi
Easton, Maryland, 142, 153, 163, 187
Edgley, Pennsylvania, 32, 60, 62, 63, 76
Elk Neck, Maryland, 103, 109, 112, 134, 245
Elkton, Maryland, 83, 106, 165
"Elliott" brand, 88
Elliott brothers, Easton, 246
    Canada goose decoy, 187
    scaup decoy, 153
    swan decoy, 163
England, 14
English, Dan, 234
    black duck decoy, 61, 145
    canvasback decoy, 78
    redhead decoy, 72
    scaup decoy, 63, 72, 73, 75, 78
English, Jack,
    black duck decoy, 64
    scaup decoy, 75
English, John, 235
    black duck decoy, 60
    bufflehead decoy, 30

goldeneye decoy, 58, 78
mallard decoy, 64
redhead decoy, 73
scaup decoy, 75
English, Mark,
    old squaw decoy, 22
    red breasted merganser decoy, 28

F

Fallston, Maryland, xi
"Fat Jaw" Ward decoy, 167, 168, 175
Fieldsboro, New Jersey, 78
Fishing Creek, Maryland, 142
Fitzpatrick, Tom,
    black duck decoy, 60
    mallard decoy, 77
    pintail decoy, 68
Fletcher, Columbus "Lum", 235
    canvasback decoy, 110
Florence, New Jersey, 30, 58, 60, 61, 63, 64, 72, 73, 75, 78, 145, 234
Folding rack decoys, 138
Forked River, New Jersey, 36
Forsyth, Sam, brant decoy, 49
Fox Island Gun Club, 173, 176
"F.S." brand, 89
Fulcher, Mitchell, 191
    redhead decoy, 228
    scaup decoy, 228

G

"G.A.E." brand, 110
Gant, Percy, bufflehead decoy, 76
"Gathered breast" Ward decoy, 173
Gibson, Paul, 83, 235
    baldpate decoy, 94
    Canada goose decoy, 115, 125, 138
    mallard decoy, 94
Glen, Captain John, 142, 235, 238, 250, 251
    black duck decoy, 148, 149
    scaup decoy, 91
Graham, John B., 81, 82, 85, 236
    black duck decoy, 99, 113, 149
    canvasback decoy, 98, 99, 103, 109, 113, 114, 135
    redhead decoy, 113, 114
    scaup decoy, 113
Grant, Henry, 31, 230
    black duck decoy, 38, 39
    Canada goose decoy, 54
    red breasted merganser decoy, 24
    scaup decoy, 46
Grant, Stanley,
    goldeneye decoy, 42
    redhead decoy, 31
    scaup decoy, 36, 46
Gray, Edson, 237

black duck decoy, 152
Canada goose decoy, 136, 151
canvasback decoy, 152
scaup decoy, 152
Green, Paul,
black duck decoy, 63
canvasback decoy, 75
scaup decoy, 76
Greenbank, Maryland, 107
Greenbank, New Jersey, 31, 36, 37, 39
Guilford, Virginia, 189
Gunning the Chesapeake, 147
Gunpowder River, 15, 16, 80

H

Hall, Severin, 109
coot decoy, 126
Hall, Will, goldeneye decoy, 33
Hammel, Bill,
red breasted merganser decoy, 28
redhead decoy, 35
Hancock, Miles, 237
baldpate decoy, 201, 203
black duck decoy, 201, 203
brant decoy, 201, 207
bufflehead decoy, 202
canvasback decoy, 204, 213
coot decoy, 203
goldeneye decoy, 202
hooded merganser decoy, 188, 189, 190
pintail decoy, 202
red breasted merganser decoy, 201, 203
redhead decoy, 204
scaup decoy, 201, 204
Hankins, I.S., redhead decoy, 32
Harborton, Virginia, 190
Hardcastle, Edmund, black duck decoy, 153
Harford County, x, xi, 15, 80
Havre de Grace, Maryland, 14, 79, 80, 81, 83, 84, 86-89, 91-98, 100, 101, 103, 104, 109-112, 115, 120, 121, 126, 127, 130, 131, 134, 137, 138, 141, 143, 145, 150, 165, 229, 232, 234, 235, 238, 239, 245-247
Hawkins, Ben, 14
Hazelhurst Club, 76
Heinefield, August George, 142, 237, 251
black duck decoy, 149
redhead decoys, 148
scaup decoy, 109
Heisler, John,
baldpate decoy, 70
black duck decoy, 60, 62

canvasback decoy, 74
Hendrickson, J. Eugene, 238
brant decoy, 50
goldeneye decoy, 29
Heverin, William, 14, 79, 238, 244
black duck decoy, 107, 108, 110, 123
canvasback decoy, 107, 108
redhead decoy, 108
scaup decoy, 108
Hillman, John, xi, 42, 46
"Hissing head" Hudson decoy, 209, 210
Hog Island, Virginia, 220, 221
Holly, James T., 83, 86, 238
black duck decoy, 86, 88, 92, 136, 137
blue wing teal decoy, 86, 141
canvasback decoy, 90, 130, 137, 242
green wing teal decoy, 87
mallard decoy, 86, 137
pintail decoy, 88, 137
redhead decoy, 88, 89, 131, 137, 239, 241
scaup decoy, 89, 97, 104
Holly, John "Daddy", 15, 79, 80, 81-83, 230, 236, 238, 239
canvasback decoy, 15, 89, 98, 130
redhead decoy, 89, 90
scaup decoy, 88, 91
Holly, John, Jr., scaup decoy, 87
Holly, John, Jr. or William, redhead decoy, 90
Holly, William, 239
Canada goose decoy, 115
scaup decoy, 90
Honga River, 16
Hooper's Island, 142, 157, 160
Hoopersville, Maryland, 142
Horner, Nathan Rowley, 243, 249
black duck decoy, 37, 39
brant decoy, 47
goldeneye decoy, 34
mallard decoy, 34, 140
red breasted merganser decoy, 25
scaup decoy, 34
"Horseshoe Keels", 81
Hudson, Ira, 14, 83, 189, 190, 243, 253
black duck decoy, 194, 197, 217, 220
brant decoy, 136, 145, 205, 206, 207, 210
bufflehead decoy, 194
Canada goose decoy, 186, 208, 209, 210, 211
canvasback decoy, 136, 145, 192, 193, 199, 210
goldeneye decoy, 194, 197

pintail decoy, 183
scaup decoy, 194, 195
Hudson pintail decoy, 218
Huff, Charles,
red breasted merganser decoy, 26
scaup decoy, 73
"Hump back" Ward decoy, 169

I

Inman, John, brant decoy, 55
Iron anchor weights, 252
Iron keels, 15, 81

J

Jackson, W. Scott, 229, 244
blue wing teal decoy, 84
canvasback decoy, 98, 106, 244
"J.B. GRAHAM" brand, 236, 237
"J. COUDON" brand, 98, 236
"J.D. POPLAR" brand, 104
Jester, Douglas, 189, 244
black duck decoy, 198, 199, 217
brant decoy, 207
Canada goose decoy, 198, 215
canvasback decoy, 199
goldeneye decoy, 200
hooded merganser decoy, 198
mallard decoy, 198
pintail decoy, 200
redhead decoy, 197, 198, 199
"J.F.W." brand, 89, 240
Jobes, Captain Harry, baldpate decoy, 150
"John Duck" decoy, 129
Johnson, Taylor, 244
black duck decoy, 37
Canada goose decoy, 51
redhead decoy, 31, 36
scaup decoy, 33, 36
Johnson, Willis, scaup decoy, 43
Joiner, Charles "Speed", 146
canvasback decoy, 147, 150
scaup decoy, 150
"J. PUSEY" brand, 121

K

Kear, Mark,
black duck decoy, 42
red breasted merganser decoy, 25
Kemp, Phil, x
scaup decoy, 91
Kent Island, ix, 15, 142
Kilpatrick, Henry,
Canada goose decoy, 52
redhead decoy, 31
"King Bee Divers", 174

King, Joe, 249
  black duck decoy, 42
  black duck decoy, D.R., 61
  brant decoy, 49
  pintail decoy, D.R., 70
  redhead decoy, 46
  scaup decoy, 32
  scaup decoy, D.R., 72
Kingsley, Dan, scaup decoy, 32
Kiptopeke, Virginia, 190
Knotts Island, North Carolina, 191,
  221, 223
Krider, John T., 80
Krider's Sporting Anecdotes, 14

L

Lakewood, New Jersey, 43
Lambert, Larry, xi
Lead weights, 81, 82
Levy, W.W.,
Lewis, Dr. Elisha J., 80
Lewis, Jim, 191
Linwood, New Jersey, 25, 42
Little Egg Harbor, 19
Litzenberg, Bob,
  canvasback decoy, 106
  redhead decoy, 106
Lockard, George, 245
Lockard, Henry, 79, 245, 248
  canvasback decoy, 103, 112, 134
  redhead decoy, 109
Locustville, Virginia, 189
Long Beach Island, New Jersey,
  38, 64
Long Island, 13, 14
Lovelock Caves, 13
Lovelock, Nevada, 13
Love Point, ix, x, 15, 91
Lowe, T. Gilbert, 245
  mallard decoy, 146
Lower Bank, New Jersey, 29, 50, 238
"L. PENNOCK" brand, 107

M

Mackey, William, 127, 159, 233, 249
Madieri, Clark,
  black duck decoy, 37, 40
  goldeneye decoy, 29
  red breasted merganser
    decoy, 26
Magothy River, 16, 146
Manahawkin, New Jersey, 20, 38, 42,
  46, 47, 49, 55, 249
Market hunter, 14
Market hunting, 16, 79
Marter, Reggie,
  black duck decoy, 63, 64
  blue wing teal decoy, 71, 141
Martin, Glenn L., 172
Mason Decoy Co., 19

red breasted merganser
  decoy, 24
Maxwell, Roy, Canada goose
  decoy, 54
McCoy, Charles, scaup decoy, 33
McCullough, J.W., 80
McGaw, Robert F., xii, 79, 83, 245
  baldpate decoy, 145
  black duck decoy, 92, 93
  canvasback decoy, 94, 112
  goldeneye decoy, 93, 136, 137
  mallard decoy, 92
  redhead decoy, 93
  scaup decoy, 91, 93, 126
McGlaughlin, Lawrence,
  black duck decoy, 62
  canvasback decoy, 76
  scaup decoy, 63
McGloughlin, John,
  mallard decoy, 71
  pintail decoy, 70
  scaup decoy, 71
Meekins, Alvin,
  bufflehead decoy, 157
  red breasted merganser
    decoy, 157, 158, 160
Middle River, 16
Miniature decoys, 116, 117
Mitchell, Madison, 83, 230, 246,
  254
  baldpate decoy, 94
  black duck decoy, 94, 95
  Canada goose decoy, 115
  canvasback decoy, 95
  mallard decoy, 95, 137, 150
  pintail decoy, 131
  redhead decoy, 95
  scaup decoy, 95
Modest Town, Virginia, 189
Morse, Bob, canvasback decoy, 227

N

Nanticoke, Maryland, 142
Newark, New Jersey, 149
New Jersey, 14, 19, 21
New York, 14
"North Carolina" brand, 240
Northeast, Maryland, 79, 126
Northeast River, 236, 238

O

Ocean City, New Jersey, 35, 38, 41,
  45, 46, 51
Ocean View, Delaware, 136, 151, 152,
  237
Old squaw, 20
Orem family swan decoy, 162
Ortley, Dipper, scaup decoy, 50
Osbourneville, New Jersey, 76
Oxford, Maryland, 142, 153, 246
Oyster, Virginia, 214, 232

P

Paiute Indians, 13
Parker, Ellis, 249
  black duck decoy, 38, 64
Parker, Lloyd,
  black duck decoy, 39
  brant decoy, 48
  Canada goose decoy, 52
  red breasted merganser
    decoy, 26, 140
  redhead decoy, 35
Parkertown, New Jersey, 26, 35,
  39, 42, 46, 48, 52, 140
Parsons, Edward T., 246
  canvasback decoy, 153
Patuxent River, 16, 146
Pearson, Edwin Ergood, 247
Pennock, Lou, 107
Perryville, Maryland, 79, 84, 92, 100,
  101, 122, 127, 136, 137, 230, 233
Philadelphia, 14, 58, 65, 80, 145
Phillips, Edward James, 247
  black duck decoy, 92
  scaup decoy, 156
Phillips, Ike, 190
Pierce, Jim, coot decoy, 120
Pittman, New Jersey, 26, 29, 37, 40
"P.K. BARNES" brand, 101, 229,
  234
Pleasantville, New Jersey,
Pocomoke River, 16
Point Pleasant, New Jersey, 31-33,
  36, 37, 51, 54, 244
Port Deposit, Maryland, 80, 86
Potomac River, 16
Price, Liberty, 42, 46
Principio, Maryland, 119
Pryor, Leonard, 248
  black duck decoy, 105, 110, 123
  canvasback decoy, 105
  pintail decoy, 105

Q

Queen Anne's County, ix
Quinn, William,
  baldpate decoy, 70
  black duck decoy, 61, 77
  gadwall decoy, 68
  mallard decoy, 69
  pintail decoy, 69
  scaup decoy, 72

R

"RECKLESS", 15, 98
  brand, 89
Reiger, George, xi
Reitz, Al,
  black duck decoy, 64
  scaup decoy, 76

Richardson, Bobby, xi
"R.M. VANDIVER", brand, 113, 239, 240
Roberts, John, scaup decoy, 73
Robinson, Ed, 150
Rock Hall, Maryland, 91, 109, 111, 142, 148, 149, 165, 235, 237, 250
Romancoke, Maryland, 142
Ruddy duck decoy, Susquehanna Flats, 129, 159
Rue, Ronald,
    black duck decoy, 145
    canvasback decoy, 155
    herring gull decoy, 155
    laughing gull decoy, 155
    scaup decoy, 155
    white wing scoter decoy, 154

S

Sabatini, Dominic, black duck decoy, 40
Salmon, Brad, black duck decoy, 38
San Domingo Club, 15
Sassafras River, 16
Scows, sailing, 15
Scratch painting technique, 83, 86, 92
Seaview, New Jersey, 50
Sellers, Robert, redhead decoy, 118
Severn River, 16, 146
Sharpless, Dr. J.J., 80, 139
"Shoe Bill" decoy, 110
Shourds, Harry Mitchell, 248
    black duck decoy, 51
    Canada goose decoy, 51
    goldeneye decoy, 35
    redhead decoy, 45
    scaup decoy, 45, 46
Shourds, Harry V., 14, 19, 20, 23, 248, 249, 253
    black duck decoy, 41, 44
    brant decoy, 48, 248
    bufflehead decoy, 76, 140
    Canada goose decoy, 53
    goldeneye decoy, 33
    old squaw decoy, 20
    red breasted merganser decoy, 23, 140
    redhead decoy, 21, 31, 44, 140
    scaup decoy, 30, 43, 44
Shourds, Harry III, brant decoy, 50
Shrewsbury, New Jersey, 26, 73
Silver Spring, Pennsylvania, 118
Sinkbox shooting, 14, 16, 79, 80
Sneak boat, Barnegat, 19
Somer's Point, New Jersey, 22, 27, 28, 77
South River, 146

"SPESUTIE I.R. & G. CLUB" brand, 87
Sprague, Chris, 25, 39, 249
    brant decoy, 49
    Canada goose decoy, 51
Stacy, North Carolina, 228
Sterling, Lloyd,
    goldeneye decoy, 174
    pintail decoy, 132
Sterling, Will and Noah, 143
Sterling, Will, goldeneye decoy, 174
Stevens, Ivey, 191
    canvasback decoy, 226
Stevensville, Maryland, 142, 232
Stumps Point, Maryland, 100, 101, 233
Sullivan, John, xi
"SUSQUEHANNA" brand, 98
Susquehanna Flats, 16, 79-83, 99, 101, 126, 141, 230
Susquehanna River, 95, 97, 118, 120, 124, 130
Swan Creek, Aberdeen, Maryland, 110, 235
Swan decoy, 162, 163, 164, 216

T

Talbot County, Maryland, 151, 153, 159, 216, 246
Taylor's Island, Maryland, 187
Thomas, Al, canvasback decoy, 110
Tilghman Island, 142
"Toling", method of hunting, 79
Travers, Captain Josiah Franklin, 250
    black duck decoy, 161
    Canada goose decoy, 161
    scaup decoy, 158
Trenton, New Jersey, 66, 67, 145, 233
Truex, Rhodes, 250
    black duck decoy, 37, 38
    brant decoy, 55
    Canada goose decoy, 52
    red breasted merganser, decoy, 26
    scaup decoy, 43
Tuckerton, 14, 19, 20, 21, 23, 25, 29, 30, 31, 33, 41, 43, 44, 48, 50, 53, 76, 140, 243, 249
Tulls Bay, North Carolina, 226
Turner, Garland, 190
Tyler, Lloyd J., 250
    pintail decoy, 132, 183
Tydings, Millard, 229

U

Updike, John,
    black duck decoy, 37, 39
    redhead decoy, 31

scaup decoy, 36
Upper Chesapeake Bay, 14, 86
Urie, Captain Jesse, 142, 235, 250
    black duck decoy, 109, 111, 149
    scaup decoy, 91

V

Vickers, John,
    black duck decoy, 149
    swan decoy, 163
Vienna, Maryland, 158, 161, 250

W

Wading River, New Jersey, 54
Walker, Wilton, canvasback decoy, 226
Walsh, Bill, xi
Walsh, Roy, 147, 153
Ward, Lemuel T. and Steve, 40, 143, 251
    baldpate decoy, 132, 136, 178
    black duck decoy, 176, 179, 180
    Canada goose decoy, 184, 185
    canvasback decoy, 133, 136, 165, 170, 171, 172, 177, 180
    goldeneye decoy, 133, 170, 173
    green wing teal, 141
    herring gull decoy, 182
    Hutchins goose decoy, 186
    mallard decoy, 133, 167, 172, 178
    old squaw decoy, 182
    pintail decoy, 18, 132, 169, 178
    redhead decoy, 133, 167, 168, 176
    scaup decoy, 133, 166, 170, 172, 173, 175
    surf scoter decoy, 182
Ward, L. Travis, Sr., 143, 251
Ward, Steve, 83, 143
Waterfield family, 191
Water Lily, North Carolina, 231
Watson, Dave "Umbrella", 189, 251
    black duck decoy, 196
    brant decoy, 145
    Canada goose decoy, 211
    canvasback decoy, 213
Watson, Milton, canvasback decoy, 105
Webb, Clarence, canvasback decoy, 165
West Creek, New Jersey, 25, 34, 37, 39, 47, 140, 243
West Mantoloking, New Jersey, 33
West River, 146
Whitaker, Nelson Price, 244
Wild fowl decoys, 13
Williams, John, 191, 251
    ruddy duck decoy, 224
Williams, John Wesley, blue wing teal decoy, 86

Willis Wharf, Virginia, 196, 207,
    211, 212, 213, 214, 216, 221
Wilson, Alexander, 13, 14, 57
Wilson, Charles T., blue wing teal
    decoy, 84, 86
Wilson Point, Maryland, 146, 150
Wilson's American Ornithology, 14
Wing duck, iron, 114, 127
Wing duck, wooden, 97, 127
Wright, Alvirah,
    canvasback decoy, 225
    redhead decoy, 225

Y

Yardley, Pennsylvania, 61, 68,
    69, 70, 72, 77
Yardville, New Jersey, 63, 75, 76

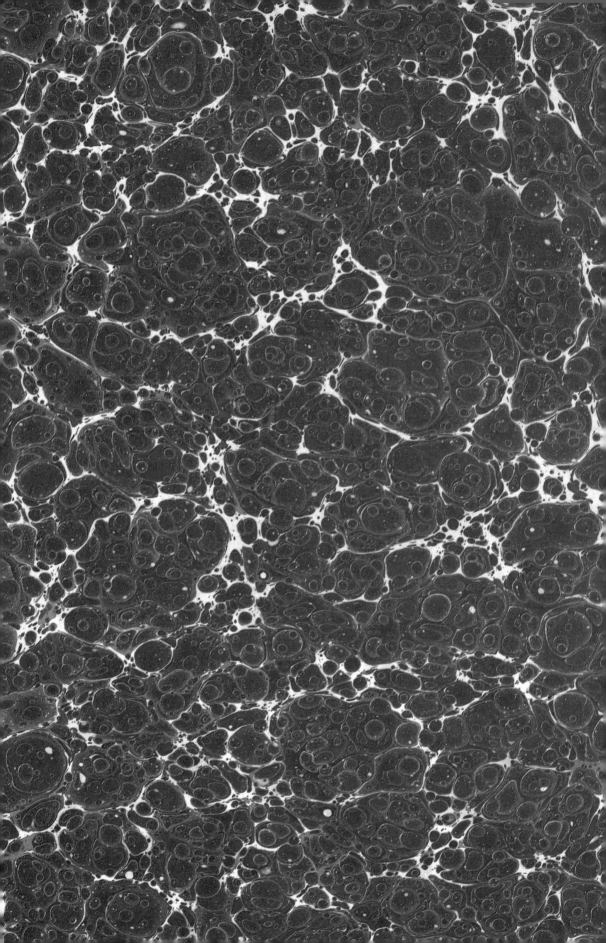